PENGUIN BOOKS

KILLING THE SACRED COWS

Ann Crittenden is an award-winning writer on economics and a former director of the Fund for Investigative Journalism in Washington, D.C. She was with *The New York Times* from 1975 to 1983, reporting on a broad range of economic issues, from international finance to domestic policy. She has also been a financial writer and foreign correspondent for *Newsweek*, a reporter for *Fortune*, a visiting lecturer at MIT and Yale, and an economics commentator for CBS News in New York. She is the author of *Sanctuary: A Story of American Conscience and the Law in Collision* (1988).

Ann Crittenden talked to economists, community organizers, small-business people, consumer activists, etc., to find out what alternatives are working now and what might work in the future. If she missed a successful enterprise or initiative in your community, please write to us and we'll try to incorporate your story in a revised edition of this book.

Please send a typed, double-spaced description to:
More Sacred Cows
Penguin USA—Department JMK
375 Hudson Street
New York, New York 10014-3657

Killing the Sacred Cows

**BOLD IDEAS
FOR A NEW
ECONOMY**

Ann Crittenden

PENGUIN BOOKS

PENGUIN BOOKS
Published by the Penguin Group
Viking Penguin, a division of Penguin Books USA Inc.,
375 Hudson Street, New York, New York 10014, U.S.A.
Penguin Books Ltd, 27 Wrights Lane,
London W8 5TZ, England
Penguin Books Australia Ltd, Ringwood,
Victoria, Australia
Penguin Books Canada Ltd, 10 Alcorn Avenue, Suite 300,
Toronto, Ontario, Canada M4V 3B2
Penguin Books (N.Z.) Ltd, 182–190 Wairau Road,
Auckland 10, New Zealand

Penguin Books Ltd, Registered Offices:
Harmondsworth, Middlesex, England

First published in Penguin Books 1993

10 9 8 7 6 5 4 3 2 1

LIBRARY OF CONGRESS CATALOGING IN PUBLICATION DATA
Crittenden, Ann.
    Killing the sacred cows: bold ideas for a new economy / Ann
Crittenden.
      p.   cm.
    ISBN 0 14 01.7321 8
    1. United States—Economic policy—1981–   I. Title.
HC106.8.C75   1993
338.973′009′048—dc20   92–27052

Printed in the United States of America

Set in New Baskerville
Designed by Brian Mulligan

Acknowledgments

Not many books owe as much to others as this one, which could have been called *Other People's Ideas*. Its debts to all those who have thought long and hard about our economic troubles, and who have come up with imaginative solutions, are tallied in the source notes at the end of this volume. But many of these never-say-die optimists, freethinkers, and problem-solvers should be singled out for special mention.

My deepest appreciation goes to Pat Choate, a fellow Texan who took time out from a European vacation to read an early version of the entire manuscript, a task no doubt akin to walking through deep snow. His creative comments are reflected throughout the book, and I can only hope that a little of his sophistication in matters of economic policy crept in as well.

Numerous others did me the invaluable favor of reading and reacting to specific chapters. I want to especially thank Robert McIntyre—that rarity, a tax expert who cares about fairness and equity; Tom Schlesinger and Jane D'Arista, among the few people in this country with a vision of a democratic financial system; Carol O'Cleireacain, finance commissioner for New York City, who vetted the pages on economically targeted investments; Barry Zigas, who knows more about how to solve our housing problems than almost anyone else in the country; Ted Kolderie, an authority on how to build meaningful choice into our public school system; Stephanie Woolhandler and Maureen Postoni, who helped guide me through the complexities of the health care debate; and Randal Forsberg, who has dared to imagine what an internationally cooperative defense policy could save us.

Many others, aside from all those whose ideas are collected in this book, provided helpful comments, useful information, and invaluable support: Robert Shapiro, Larry Mishel, Eileen Applebaum, Derek Shearer, Wallace Katz, Deborah Miller Davidow, Michael Telson, Charles Moskos, Mike Peabody, Bob Borsage, Ken Galston, Jim Benn, Greg Leroy, Ralph Nader, Bob Friedman, Scott Hodge, Jamie Galbraith, Martin Tremble, Michael Piore, Timothy Saasta, Phil Burgess, Doug Ross, Steve Rohde, Fred Block, Steve Kest, Deepak Bhargava, Jim Hightower, Heidi Hartman, Dan Morgan, Jim Chapin, Bill Ayres, Gerald Epstein, Joanna Pruess, my agent Joseph Spieler, my editor, Nan Graham, and her assistant, Courtney Hodell, at Viking, the most congenial taskmasters one could hope to have, and, not least, the members of my workout group, who provided daily physical and social sustenance while my mind was doing hard time, trying to solve all the problems of the world.

Contents

Introduction

I've always loved ideas. A few years ago, I was approached to be the "issues" director for a Democratic presidential hopeful. Eventually, I declined the offer, but during the courtship I attended a few fund-raisers for the aspirant. At one such gathering, I was introduced as "Ann Crittenden—she's interested in *ideas*." The slightly wondrous tone of the comment, akin to "she's interested in Romanian cuisine," left no doubt that my enthusiasm verged on the eccentric in the money-dominated world of Washington politics.

But that was then—1983—and this is now, and times sure have changed in ten short years. Then, we were just beginning the great experiment to see whether we could marry nineteenth-century Gilded Age capitalism with late-twentieth-century hedonism and risk aversion. We could, and what a charming family the union produced: regulatory negligence and the S&L mess, go-for-broke government spending and a mountain of debt, a corporate structure that discourages long-term investment, growing inequalities, and the beginnings of class warfare. This is what can happen when you don't read history, which at least teaches you what an anachronism is.

So where does all that leave us and the economy today, and what can we do about it? When I first began this book, in early 1992, I had a sense that a Big Thaw was about to begin in the United States, after years in an ideological deep freeze. Like Sleeping Beauty, people were waking up and asking, "Where am I? What happened? Where's my health insurance? Where's my pension? Where's my bank? Where's my job? How is my kid going to go to college?"

Meanwhile, the rest of the world had not been taking a nap, and when Sleeping Beauty looked around, she saw that everything had changed beyond recognition. The Soviet Union was gone, the Chinese had turned capitalist, our old enemies in Eastern Europe were clamoring to join our side, and our old friends in Japan and Western Europe were out-competing us in the global economy. It all added up to the most urgent demand for fresh thinking and a fundamental reappraisal of our accustomed way of doing things that we have faced in fifty years.

So this book became a compilation of the best ideas I could find on what we could do to put things right in the American economy. As it turned out, there was no shortage of good, original thinking on the subject. Successful political and economic experiments are popping up all over the States, many of them documented in David Osbourne's influential book *Reinventing Government*. Citizens' initiatives and consumer organizations have produced changes in bank lending, in school organization, in the ways communities react to plant closings. From the University of California in Davis to the University of Notre Dame to Bard College and Boston College and places in between, academics are coming up with blueprints for economic and financial reform. Think tanks and policy institutes on the right, left, and center continue to pour out ideas; and special commissions deliver well-crafted, practical proposals and reports that enjoy a day's publicity before falling into a black hole.

All these sources were mined for this book. I also drew upon dozens of interviews with scholars, businessmen, financiers, politicians, activists, and just plain people all around the country and from all points on the ideological spectrum.

(Although one reader of an early version of the manuscript wrote in his notes, "Ann, I have noted that while you mention several good ideas from Clinton, Perot, and others, I have difficulty remembering any that have been proposed by the Administration. Is this an oversight, deliberate, or merely a reflection of an intellectual vacuum in the government?"

Without putting too fine a point on it—the latter. If you love ideas, it is hard to love the Bush administration.)

Some of the freshest ideas came from the op-ed sections and letters to the editor of several major publications, including *The New York Times, The Washington Post, The Wall Street Journal*, and *Barron's*.

Few of the best ideas fit into the traditional mold of the throw-them-a-bone, big-government Democrats or the let-them-eat-cake, big-business, big-military Republicans. The either-or categories of "private enterprise" and "public sector" are passé; the economic reality is totally mixed.

One can encourage entrepreneurialism with tax incentives and cut the tax subsidies of big corporations. One can stimulate productive private investment by using government money as a carrot and encourage more productive bank lending by using government mandates as a stick. One can introduce choice into education and still preserve the integrity of the public schools. One can have national health insurance *and* private health care. One can cut entitlements—of those who can afford it—and extend the safety net. One can build needed public infrastructure and find ways to get private money to pay for some of it. One can make able-bodied welfare recipients work and get well-heeled recipients of government handouts off the dole. One can cut our military budget to the bone and improve our national security with global peace-keeping, better worker training, big investments in commercial R&D, and a stiff gasoline tax.

Many if not most of these eclectic prescriptions are vehemently opposed by some industry, trade association, or special-interest lobby. But many have also been successfully carried out abroad or at the more innovative state and local levels, where interest groups have learned to work together in a healthy political give-and-take that is utterly missing from Washington. Given support by wise national leadership, any number of these provocative and sensible ideas are ready to roll into service.

The prospect belies the fashionable pessimism that "there is nothing we can do," that "our hands are tied because of the deficit," and that "Americans are going to have to make major sacrifices" to put the economy back on the right track. Implementing solutions won't be easy. The political process, maybe even the public itself, has not permitted bold action. Change will require sacrifices, but not from anyone who can't afford them. To assert otherwise is a counsel of despair that amounts to a defense of the status quo. This is a rich, diverse country full of imagination and energy. We have on hand the solutions we need to give new life to the economy; we need the courage to try them.

There are certain watershed periods in which taking a chance on bold action is less dangerous than holding back or proceeding with caution. This is one of those times, and the American people know it.

It is as if we were in 1933 and 1945 at the same time: Just as our economic system is staggering under the weight of past folly and excess, an inviting new postwar world is opening up. The only thing the two crosscurrents have in common is their demand for leadership and for the kind of bold initiatives that we had during the Depression and after World War II.

The closer historical analogy is probably 1933. Franklin Roosevelt began his first term with a relatively modest set of economic proposals, but as the crisis deepened, one radically new program after another was put into place. Few were invented outright by the new president's brain trust. Some had already been tried in New York State by Governor Al Smith; others were untested proposals whose time had finally come. Many if not most of those initiatives are still with us: not just the familiar New Deal safety net, but such innovations as the industrial revenue bond, invented by Mississippi in 1936 to attract business, and public housing, first built in 1937 for families temporarily in distress.

This book describes daring new proposals similar to these Depression-born initiatives and to postwar innovations like the G.I. Bill, federally insured home mortgages, and the World Bank. These include a "New World Order" on corporate taxation; a *new* G.I. bill; a national service corps; a national apprenticeship system; an American Investment Bank to rebuild our transportation system and decaying public facilities; an industrial-extension service to spread technological innovation to small businesses (based on the already hugely successful agricultural-extension service for small farmers); and a new system of "people's banks," financing community development and low-income home ownership, that can do for small borrowers and businesses and home buyers what VA and FHA loans have done in the past.

We can't do much of any of this unless we drastically cut the "defense" budget and eliminate wasteful subsidies to the well-off. And we can't cut the budget unless we simultaneously initiate at least some of these reforms to make up for the shock to millions of government employees. This is the Grand Trade-off that will enable us to make the transition to a postwar civilian economy that is globally competitive. The American people clearly want this kind of drastic change, and they said so in poll after poll during the 1992 presidential campaign.

Even such bastions of the establishment as the Harvard Business School recognize the need for dramatic change. In *Capital Choices*, a thoughtful report on American corporate investment prepared for the White House Council on Competitiveness, Professor Michael Porter writes that the U.S. system of capital allocation requires a "systemic change. . . . America must avoid the tendency to tinker at the margin. The widespread concern and dissatisfaction with the *status quo* suggests that systemic reform may be possible."

Whether change will occur is another question. The bureaucrats in American big business and government are the mirror image of their old adversaries in the Kremlin. (An investment letter I received in the mail recently had on its cover a picture of the Capitol under the headline THE LAST BASTION OF SOCIALISM.) We too have a discredited elite that would rather cling to tired, timid little thoughts and conventional bromides—and to its own considerable privileges—than lead an American *perestroika*, despite the obvious need for a shake-up.

But if change can come to Eastern Europe, it can happen here. It has to.

Remember the "It's Morning in America" campaign? Well, now we have to deal with the hangover. This book is intended to be a wake-up call with some real remedies.

∎ ∎ ∎

There are several unmistakable themes discernible in the kinds of proposals making the rounds today; certain straws in the winds of change. On these, the nation is in surprising agreement.

The first—and this is no news to anyone who has been following the economic debate—is that we have to invest much more in educating our work force and reconstructing our public facilities. The country has been like a family that borrowed money to buy fast cars and vacations while letting the roof fall in and forgetting to send the kids to college.

More than twenty years ago, the World Bank realized that developing countries couldn't achieve economic prosperity unless what was called "basic human needs" were met; and ever since, the Bank has financed education, clean water, and housing along with dams and roads and power plants. This support is not rooted in bleeding-heart liberalism but in a calculated understanding that a modern economy cannot prosper without a well-educated, well-trained, well-fed, and well-housed population.

To say this is to state the obvious. No one believes that the Europeans have such a high standard of living because they have cheap labor, or that the Japanese are getting rich by neglecting their people's education. Obviously, "human capital," as economists sometimes call people, is a country's greatest natural resource, even in the relatively well endowed United States.

We finally seem to have realized that education *is* economic development; that neglecting our human resources is as destructive as neglecting our environment or our industrial base; that investing in people, from infancy through old age, is as hardheaded as investing in iron and steel or bricks and mortar. You don't have to be an economist to recognize that better training, particularly for the "neglected half"—the lowest 50 percent of our students—translates into greater productivity, a higher standard of living, less income inequality, and more social stability for the country as a whole.

This message was stated loud and clear a few years ago by the bipartisan Commission on the Skills of the American Work force, chaired by two former secretaries of labor: Bill Brock, a Republican, and Ray Marshall, a Democrat. Their influential 1990 report, *America's Choice*, warned that the United States faces an urgent decision on whether it is to become a nation of unskilled low-wage workers competing in a "race to the bottom" with Third World labor—the path it is currently taking—or a nation of highly skilled workers producing quality goods that can compete anywhere in the world.

The United States is already well along the low road, as the wages of millions of blue-collar workers fall further and further behind those of the educated. At the end of that road lies an inefficient use of labor, a less productive economy, even deeper divisions of class and race in America than already exist, and a potentially explosive political reaction. A number of the ideas in this book show how we can avoid that impoverishing, profoundly undemocratic path.

I have also discovered almost unanimous agreement that we need to step up our economic investment in public goods and our emotional investment in common goals. Our economic debate is often cast as a struggle between investment and consumption, a drama ultimately played out by an individual with the personal choice to spend or to save. But what ever happened to *public* consumption? The mirror image of our overgrown bureaucracies is our isolation as individuals, separated from one another by an absence of civic institutions and civic vision. The lack of a "vision thing" is at the heart of our economic problems. If we could recognize that we are all in this together, that our shared efforts could build a stronger system, that all our wants don't have to be personal and material, the crudest kind of private gratification—what we couldn't do for ourselves *and* the economy!

We would understand that public investments and public commitments do not entail "sacrifice." We could have faster mass transportation instead of new Nikes or Rollerblades, cleaner air and water instead of the latest video game. We could forgo a new Jacuzzi for the sake of fewer homeless in our streets. We could participate in service corps that took care of kids and old people, planted trees, manned bookmobiles, helped the police, and did all the other things society needs but cannot afford unless everyone pitches in.

In other words, if we could accept a broader, less narcissistic definition of prosperity, we could all be better off. Now that communism is dead, maybe we can lose our fear of communal solutions.

Another thread running through many of the best ideas I uncovered has been called "reinventing government," but it could just as well be called "reinventing business."

Much has been written recently about "the new paradigm" of public-private partnerships to solve economic and environmental problems. The idea is that the government should act as a facilitator, or catalyst, to encourage and prod private markets, institutions, and capital to do as much of the job as possible. This implies a much more sophisticated targeting of government resources than the outmoded government-can-handle-everything, let's-just-throw-money-at-it attitude. This book contains several suggestions on how to leverage government money to stimulate greater private investment in, among other things, infrastructure, affordable housing, and civilian research and technology.

The only problem with this commendable approach is that it slights the reality that the national government is the abject creature of the most powerful vested interests. Many of the worst failures in our economy today are not of government per se but of a political economy dominated by private industry. How can we use the government to prod the private sector to serve the public interest if we don't *control* the government?

In the past decade, corporations have shed employee pension funds, cut health benefits, discarded workers, abandoned communities, defeated a strong energy policy, subverted the environmental laws, thrown publicly guaranteed bank deposits down speculative ratholes, overcharged the military billions of dollars, and *still* enjoyed enormous tax breaks and public contracts.

If we really want to reinvent government, we have to take it back first, as Jerry Brown put it, and stop the pillaging. We need to reinvent business. *Capital Choices* concluded that the American system of investment "may come closer to optimizing short-term private returns. However, the Japanese and German systems appear to come closer to optimizing long-term private and social returns."

This is the direction in which we need to head. We have to understand that a capitalism that tries to move forward in a hurry while leaving vast numbers of people out of the picture isn't going anywhere.

Which leads to the last and most controversial theme I've discerned. We must arrest the growing inequality in the economy and place a higher value on *fairness*, an idea so basic that children of two and three understand it. Fair means that we don't give billions of dollars' worth of tax-free subsidies to the rich while begrudging assistance to poor children. Fair means that we don't allocate credit to those who don't need it and deny it to those who do. Fair, it is not widely enough understood, means greater economic growth and stability.

Economic fairness and economic growth and competitiveness are not locked in one of those ugly trade-offs, like good food and fat. People work harder when they know that their bosses' jobs and salaries are on the line as much as theirs are.

Productivity increases when people know that their opinions carry real weight and that their rewards will be related to their companies' gains. Citizens accept sacrifices more readily if they know that everyone has to tighten their belts.

This last is crucial, for the American economy is in a deep debt crisis that to be overcome is going to require a massive reallocation of resources and a keen sense of shared purpose.

Just how dire the crisis is can be measured by what it now takes to keep the system afloat. During the past decade, short-term interest rates have dropped by nearly 80 percent, from a peak of 21 percent to below 4 percent, and the government has been spending four dollars for every three dollars collected—and economic growth is still sluggish.

By the late summer of 1992, persistent deficit spending was running at the rate of $11,500 a second and had produced a national debt of $4 trillion. All the personal federal income tax paid by people west of the Mississippi fails to pay even the interest on that sum (which doesn't even include the government's contingent liabilities arising from federal guarantees on everything from student loans to corporate pensions).

Interest on the debt now eats up $200 billion a year—all of it going to relatively well-off holders of Treasury securities instead of being invested in factories, education, roads, and communications. If deficits were being incurred to make these kinds of productive investments, then the red ink would not be so worrisome. But the spending is paying for consumption, for a myriad things—like the salaries of military personnel overseas and rising health costs—that do not make the economy grow and prosper.

Most economists now agree that something must be done to stop the mortgaging of America's future prosperity. This something will entail major reductions and reallocations of government spending, and tax increases as well. (One estimate making the rounds is a cut in federal spending by $50 billion to $100 billion and a tax increase of 5 to 10 percent—roughly another $50 billion to $100 billion—the equivalent of 1 to 2 percent of personal income.) It won't be pretty, to paraphrase Ross Perot, but it isn't the end of the world, and it had better be done fairly.

The sacrifices can't all come from average American families, whose household purchasing power is now lower than it was in 1979. And more pain can't be inflicted on the almost 36 million poor people in this country, whose ranks have been increasing steadily for the past two years. Unless people and corporations who can afford it bite the bullet and help end the budget crisis—and this book has many ideas on how they might do that—it's a safe bet we won't solve any of our economic problems.

I am well aware of the criticisms that can be leveled against a book like this. What is the use of compiling a wish list of what-might-bes when our politics are paralyzed? Why draw up proposals for change when vested interests will never let the slightest reforms occur? How futile can you get? One acquaintance suggested that this book be called *Let's Pretend*.

Author Wiliam Greider, who believes that "the roots of democratic decay" are so deep that "the system will not be cured by an election or two"—in this he is no doubt right—argues that economic and political change will not come from books. "A democratic insurgency does not begin with ideas, as intellectuals presume, or even with great political leaders who seize the moment. It originates among the ordinary people who find the will to engage themselves with their surrounding reality and to question the conflict between what they are told and what they see and experience . . . questions that may lead them into action."

But what provides the mysterious spark that enables people to find the will to engage? What spurs them into action after they have begun to question, and after they have concluded that something is rotten in the system?

I believe that part of the answer *is* ideas: the knowledge that there *are* solutions waiting on the other side of an oppressive, depressing status quo. New ideas are empowering to the subjugated and dangerous to the powers that be—why else would the writers, the professors, and the priests be the first to go under a dictatorship? The awareness that there are solutions, not just problems, makes it easier to get organized. The knowledge that alternatives exist somewhere else gives one the courage to challenge the way things are here. A fresh vision can galvanize people who desire change into putting that desire into motion.

John Locke did that for the American revolutionaries; Jean-Jacques Rousseau, and the American example, did it for the French. Karl Marx did it for more people than we might like to think. More recently, Simone de Beauvoir's *The Second Sex* and Betty Friedan's *The Feminine Mystique* did it for women—myself included. I'll never forget the powerful, elated sense of possibility I felt after reading Beauvoir. And like it or not, the Ayatollah, with his evocation of a "pure" Islam, overthrew the Shah more surely than any armored divisions.

Closer to the subject at hand, both Woodrow Wilson and Franklin Roosevelt could trace their programs back to the Progressive movement, which found much of *its* inspiration in Edward Bellamy's 1888 book, *Looking Backward*. Bellamy painted a prescient picture of a kinder, gentler industrial society, imagining Social Security, a fifty-hour week, child care, health care, and public education through high school. His book became one of the best-sellers of the nineteenth century, and helped foment the democratic insurgency of the early twentieth century.

Ideas do matter. Of course, *Killing the Sacred Cows* is not a grand vision of a new world; it is merely a collection of measures we can take to improve the one we have. But they add up to compelling evidence that solutions to our economic problems do exist if only we can muster the will to apply them.

"One person with a belief is a social power equal to ninety-nine who have only interests."

The quote is from John Stuart Mill, and it adorns the publications of the Progressive Policy Institute, a Washington think tank associated with the Democratic Leadership Council. Usually described as "centrist," and clearly careful not to step on too many powerful toes, the Institute has nonetheless published a number of humane, commonsense proposals, several of which are referred to in this book.

Ironically, common sense may in fact be radical today, for it challenges the ideological myths that have clouded our vision for so long and enables people to see through the smog of special pleading that passes these days for public discussion.

If commonsense solutions can be joined with the radical power of imagination—the power to imagine a system of money and credit that operates for the benefit of ordinary people, the power to imagine quality education and training for every child, the power to imagine a capitalism that provides work and a chance to build assets to every able-bodied person—then we might just muster enough optimism to overcome the pessimism of a cynical society.

In the coming years, we are going to need all the bright ideas we can come up with. We're going to need to open ourselves to uninhibited questioning, flights of imagination, and trial and error. We're going to have to get smart and be humble, and learn from other countries' experiences. We're going to have to listen to unexpected voices previously ignored, and pick everybody's brains. We no longer have the luxury of dogmatism, like the rulers of seventeenth-century Catholic Spain, a powerful but declining society sometimes compared to our own; for arrogance and the warm comforts of ideology are only for powers headed over the hills into the sunset—as the Communists, too, found out.

=======

Two Ways to Cure the Deficit

RAISE TAXES: WHAT THE POLITICIANS AREN'T TELLING YOU

THE PRICE OF A CIVILIZED SOCIETY

Oliver Wendell Holmes once said that taxes are the price we pay for a civilized society; not very many Americans would agree with him. We've never been fond of contributing to the upkeep of the state, a sentiment that goes at least as far back as the Boston Tea Party. The United States ranks twenty-fourth among twenty-four industrialized countries in taxes collected as a percentage of GNP, and still we complain.

Perhaps the reason is that we get so much less for our tax dollars than do Western Europeans or the Japanese, who enjoy clean cities, free education, and universal medical care for their contributions to the public till.

What's more, the common perception that most Americans have—that their taxes have been going *up*—is correct. A couple with income of $50,000 saw their federal taxes rise from 18 percent in 1977 to 19.3 percent in 1990. People in the lowest income group had a 3 percent rise in effective income taxes (the taxes actually paid), from 10 percent to 13.1 percent.

Only the rich did well in this period. A couple with $200,000 of income enjoyed a *drop* in their effective overall tax rate, from 30.2 percent to 21.7 percent in the last fifteen years. The top 1 percent of families not only gained more income and wealth than any other group in America during the past fifteen years, they paid a lower percentage of it to the government in taxes.

In light of these trends, even H&R Block Inc., the country's biggest tax-preparation firm, has strongly recommended restoring greater progressivity to the tax code.

For those of you who are curious as to what kind of revenues higher taxes on the highest income earners would generate, the answer is: plenty.

Currently, the top marginal tax rate on individuals is 31 percent (although until 1996, some high-income taxpayers face effective marginal tax rates of 34 percent as their exemptions and deductions are reduced).

Congress passed a bill in March 1992 to raise the top tax rate on the top 1 percent of taxpayers to 36 percent (for purposes of comparison, Canada's highest tax bracket is 45 percent). The top rate would begin at $140,000 for joint returns. This change, which was vetoed by President Bush, would have generated $53 billion over five years.

Even assuming higher state and local taxes, high-income taxpayers would still have been better off than they were before the 1980s, a decade in which their income rose significantly.

To get at some of that extraordinary income gain at the very highest levels, Congress also passed (and President Bush also vetoed) a so-called "millionaire's surtax." An expanded version, imposing a 10 percent surtax on taxes attributable to income above $500,000 and an additional 10 percent surtax above $1 million, would generate $25 billion more in five years. Together with the tax-rate increase, the two surtaxes would result in a maximum income tax rate of about 43.5 percent.

Those supporting a surtax say that they simply want to restore progressivity to the tax structure and place the tax burden where it would impose no hardship. Eventually, the demands of bringing the federal budget deficit into line and finding money for the domestic programs we need may require these kinds of taps on individuals. Personally, I'd rather leave the personal income tax rates alone and raise revenues from the rich another way. The big problem with the federal budget—and the real injustice—is not the tax rate but the out-and-out tax subsidies that corporations, industries, and well-off individuals receive from the government.

Instead of asking, "Should we raise taxes to reduce the budget deficit and pay for the domestic programs we need?" we should ask, "How can we eliminate subsidies, tax breaks, and government giveaways to those who don't need them?"

Or, better yet, "How can we stop spending our hard-earned tax dollars on rich and powerful special interests so that we can use the money more productively?"

Not "No new taxes," but "No more tax breaks."

Posing the problem this way makes the task of raising revenues much more palatable, but not easier. The chances of eliminating tax subsidies for the folks who write the tax laws are roughly equal to the chances of finding an open suitcase of one-hundred-dollar bills on 34th St. In other words, it would be a miracle.

Even mentioning the topic of higher corporate taxes is utterly, completely taboo. That is why we hear so much talk about higher taxes on *individuals*: Even wealthy people don't have as much clout as this country's business behemoths. Sadly, it is not even relevant in many circles that getting rid of some of the more twisted kinks in the tax code would be downright healthy for the economy.

GETTING CORPORATIONS OFF WELFARE

"Japanese companies pay big taxes, and you can see how it's ruined their economy," wryly notes Robert S. McIntyre, director of Citizens for Tax Justice, a nonprofit research organization supported by unions and public-interest groups.

But corporate taxation is one aspect of the Japanese economy that American business doesn't like to talk about much. On the contrary, U.S. corporations were busy during the 1980s *lowering* their effective tax rate, a goal that was easy, given their intimate relations with a "government by and for the highest bidder," as Seattle activist Peg Prudeau put it.

The top statutory rate on corporations was lowered from 46 percent to 34 percent in 1986, and few companies even pay that much, given the virtually endless possibilities for them to reduce their taxable income. The effective corporate rate is roughly 25 percent. As a fraction of national output, corporate taxes amount to 2.6 percent in the United States (eleventh among the industrialized countries), compared with 7.5 percent in Japan.

No one would want to squelch the derring-do and animal spirits of the entrepreneur, but multibillion-dollar tax avoidance by multibillion-dollar corporations is an entirely different matter. Where is it written that creative accounting and Washington corruption should allow major companies to avoid paying their share of the burden of maintaining the federal government? We're so starry-eyed that we even let Hollywood studios claim a loss on movies that gross $300 million. Enough already.

What follows is a list of the most dispensable corporate tax expenditures. Not only could we live without these tax breaks—without them, we would have a fairer, more economically sound tax system.

■   ■   ■

THE BORROWING SUBSIDY

In our present system, a company can borrow money from a bank, use those funds to buy up the shares of another company, and deduct the interest payments on that debt from its income taxes.

A company that is afraid of being acquired can borrow money to buy up its own shares—a wholly unproductive investment—and, again, deduct the interest payments on the debt.

We could do the economy a gigantic favor by eliminating the full deductibility of corporate interest payments.

Full deductibility favors corporate borrowing over issuing stock: When companies distribute stock dividends, the income is taxed once as corporate profits and again as investor income. But when earnings are paid out as interest on corporate debt, companies can deduct those interest payments.

Thanks to this favorable tax treatment of borrowing, the U.S. Treasury in effect subsidized the frenzy of acquisitions and leveraged buyouts during the 1980s, and the concomitant destruction of companies and jobs all over the country. From 1985 to 1990, more than $1 trillion in new corporate indebtedness was incurred, and companies spent another $54 billion to buy back and retire their own stock. This is now costing the Treasury some $20 billion to $30 billion a year in lost corporate taxes, and has left hundreds of once prosperous companies staggering under huge debt loads.

A recent survey of forty-one of *Fortune* magazine's "deals of the year" between 1985 and 1990 found half the cited companies in poor or failing health, some in bankruptcy. The borrowing deduction, designed to help businesses buy new equipment and build new plants, has become instead a tool to help businesses destroy one another. In effect, the government is encouraging the weakening of corporate balance sheets, and taxpayers are underwriting the increased fragility of the financial system.

The merger and acquisition frenzy is over for now, but a couple of timely tax changes could help prevent its recurrence. If just the interest on debt to purchase stock in excess of $5 million were no longer deductible, and companies were not allowed to write off "goodwill" and similar intangible assets of acquired companies, the revenue gain to the nation would be $9 billion over five years.

The interest deduction was originally limited to investment in plants and equipment—nothing else. We should go back to that original purpose.

THE ADVERTISING SUBSIDY
The tax laws allow companies to write off the full costs of advertising in the year the expense occurs. Why not treat some of those expenses as a gradual deduction, since advertising can contribute to brand recognition that lasts for years? If only 20 percent of the spending for advertising were amortized and gradually deducted on a straight-line basis over four years, the Treasury would raise roughly $18 billion in the first five years, with declining gains after that.

Heavy advertisers might decide, of course, that all those expenses weren't quite worth it. But that would give a boost to their smaller, less well heeled competitors.

THE PERRIER SUBSIDY
Remember the two- and three-martini lunch? It has been eliminated by a change in tastes and a cut in the deduction for business meals and entertainment. Now companies can write off only 80 percent of those costs. If that deduction were re-

duced to 50 percent, we could raise revenues by $18 billion over five years.

If you have ever lunched in the right places in, say, Washington, Los Angeles, or Chicago, and surveyed the sea of mostly male executives consuming twenty-five-dollar entrees and five-dollar coffees, it may have occurred to you that the national interest doesn't require this kind of deduction. Let's cut it to 50 percent and call it the EAT (Equalization of Alimentary Taxes) Reform.

THE PUERTO RICAN SUBSIDY

Another candidate for a quick mercy killing is the possessions tax credit, labeled "the mother of all tax shelters" by Democratic senator David Pryor of Arkansas. This gem effectively exempts from federal tax all income of U.S. corporations that is earned in Puerto Rico (our biggest and closest "possession").

The original idea was to create jobs on the impoverished island by giving companies tax breaks to set up manufacturing operations there. It worked: A study in 1987 did show that 82 percent of the manufacturing jobs on the island were in possessions corporations. But the credit has ended up bestowing lavish rewards on some industries—particularly the already prosperous prescription-drug business—way out of proportion to the number of jobs they have created. Pharmaceutical manufacturers received 54 percent of the possessions tax credit benefits in 1987 but accounted for only 18 percent of the possessions corporations' jobs. According to the General Accounting Office, for each $26,000 job they created, the drug companies netted $71,000 in tax breaks (a figure the drug companies dispute).

Jobs aside, the primary incentive of the tax break is not to encourage investment in plants and equipment but to reallocate artificially the income from intangible assets developed in the United States—a classic tax giveaway handed to an industry that charges Americans 50 to 60 percent more for its drugs than consumers are charged anywhere else in the industrialized world.

Repeal of the credit would produce $15 billion over five years.

THE MULTINATIONAL LOOPHOLES

Advocates of fair taxation agree that it is time to adopt a whole new approach to taxing multinational corporations. The current system is irrational, hideously complex, invites massive tax avoidance, and encourages U.S. companies to locate plants and jobs offshore—not exactly what our tax system ought to be doing at the moment. According to Robert McIntyre of Citizens for Tax Justice, multinational companies' failure to pay taxes on the profits they earn in the United States costs the Treasury $10 billion to $20 billion *a year*—which even by Washington standards amounts to real money.

Foreign companies love our little tax haven. Between 1979 and 1986, the total receipts of foreign-controlled domestic corporations grew by 55 percent in constant dollars, while their reported income fell by 118 percent and their income-tax payments declined by 18 percent. Boy, those must have been poorly managed companies! Compared to U.S.-owned companies, foreign-controlled corporations reported only half as much taxable income as a share of either receipts or assets in 1986.

In fact, fewer than four out of ten foreign-owned companies in the United States reported *any* net income in 1986. Overall, foreign companies here reported *negative* net income and paid a paltry $3 billion in federal income taxes.

Multinational companies spirit their U.S. profits away in a number of ways. A Congressional Budget Office report in May 1992 declared that "increasingly aggressive transfer pricing by . . . multinational companies [that is, shifting profits earned here into a lower tax jurisdiction] may be one source of the shortfall in corporate tax payments in recent years."

The good old interest deduction allows another technique: Foreign companies finance their U.S. operations with debt, which allows them to pay high interest charges to the banks in their parent countries and write off the payments on their U.S. taxes. And to raise expenses in the U.S., they also load consulting fees, royalty fees, and the like onto their American operations.

Surely we could find a way for the multinationals to contribute just a bit more for the pleasure of serving our vast market of 250 million big-spending consumers.

We need a New World Order for taxes—a complete overhaul of the rules governing the international allocation of profits. Instead of the unworkable current system, which tries to convert intracompany prices into theoretical "arm's length transactions," we should go to a formula approach. Each country would tax a multinational company based on the share of its sales, assets, and payroll in that country. This is the same method that some states here have tried to use to determine the income taxes owed them by multinationals.

This "unitary tax" idea is simple, clear, and fair, and requires neither mucking around in a company's books nor Byzantine accounting methods. The estimated revenue gain for the United States if we could move to such a system: $23 billion over five years.

The only trouble is that the multinational companies, which move and shake national governments, would go bananas. In the mid-1980s, the state of California gave up on the unitary tax approach after the Sony Corporation, the Electronics Industry Association of Japan, and the British government practically threatened to tear the arms off the governor and the state legislature. The cost to the people of California? An estimated $300 million a year, at least.

THE RUNAWAY PLANT SUBSIDIES

The current tax code doubly encourages companies to locate plants in lower tax jurisdictions abroad. The first inducement is the foreign tax credit, by which an American corporation is given a dollar-for-dollar credit against U.S. taxes for any taxes paid to a foreign government.

So far, so good, although some critics point out that because taxes paid to states are only *deductible* from taxable income, thereby reducing federal taxes by only thirty-four cents on the dollar (the corporate tax rate is 34 percent), this foreign-tax-credit program amounts to an actual incentive to go offshore. But the law goes further, and allows companies to use the tax credits earned by paying taxes in high-tax countries like Germany to offset U.S. taxes on repatriated profits from low-tax countries like Ireland. You may be confused, but American companies aren't: It's why so many of them locate factories in Ireland.

The tax credit also allows companies to defer indefinitely taxes on foreign income earned by their subsidiaries abroad; technically, until the profits are repatriated. This encourages the reinvestment of such earnings overseas rather than back home. It is hard to see how all this serves the national interest at this stage of the global economic game.

Disallowing these two tax breaks would save the Treasury $1 billion over five years and could save an uncounted number of American jobs.

THE FOREIGNERS' SUBSIDY

Did you know that all interest income earned on U.S. investments by foreigners is tax exempt? Under a Reagan-era law, foreigners—including *anyone* with an offshore bank account —enjoy a tax advantage not available to Americans. Typically, this interest income is not reported to foreigners' home governments, either. As a result, according to Citizens for Tax

Justice, the United States has become a major international tax haven. If a 5 percent tax were imposed on interest earned by foreigners in the United States on loans to companies and the U.S. government, the revenue gain would be $11 billion over five years, even if the tax were waived for those who reported the income to their home government.

THE LOSERS' SUBSIDY

Of all the tax breaks dreamed up to help business, one of the most abused is the "net-operating-loss deduction," a complicated tax provision that cost the U.S. Treasury *$102 billion* between 1980 and 1988.

The basic idea is that companies can carry losses forward in time, offsetting them against future taxable income, *and* carry losses back three years and collect a *refund* on taxes already paid.

Tax experts argue that there is nothing wrong with the "tax-loss carryforwards," as they are called in the trade. They can help companies in cyclical businesses (like autos) smooth out their earnings and make it through the lean years. They also give a break to young high-tech companies that run losses in their early years from spending on research and product development.

But what economic purpose is served by the "carrybacks," which enable unprofitable companies to collect tax refunds?

If individuals could play the carryback game, it would work like this: If you lost your job this year and were living off your savings and unemployment benefits, you could obtain a refund on the money you paid in taxes last year. Not so bad.

But of course, individuals *can't* do this, only corporations can. And in the 1980s, they badly abused the practice.

Back in 1969, companies wrote off $2.5 billion in net operating losses, or 3 percent of their taxable income. By 1988, those deductions came to $51.4 billion, or 13 percent of taxable income. It pays to take a closer look at a boondoggle of this magnitude.

The net-operating-loss deduction allows companies to acquire other, money-losing companies and use the tax loss to cut their own tax bills. General Electric, for example, has a leasing subsidiary that buys other companies' net operating losses at a discount; these are then applied against the big, profitable company's taxable income.

The "NOL" thus inflates the value of bad or badly managed businesses. New owners of failed S&Ls, for example, can convert into tax savings the fraudulent losses incurred by previous owners. The failure and bailout of one Texas S&L, Guaranty Federal, is expected to cost taxpayers $4.5 billion, including tax breaks worth more than a half billion dollars— even though the S&L's owners, responsible for those losses, went to jail.

Can you think of a sweeter way to reduce the deficit than by repealing this break? Considering the hordes of lawyers and accountants specializing in tax matters, it is striking that no one seems to have calculated what getting rid of carrybacks and the transferability of tax losses would save the Treasury. Rest assured that it has to amount to a few billion dollars a year.

■　■　■

The tax reforms suggested in these last few pages could generate roughly $100 billion over five years. The corporate tax rate would *still* be lower here than in our competitor nations, and several serious distortions in the American economy would be eliminated. That most of these reforms are virtually never discussed is a disconcerting indication of the dominance of corporate power over our political and intellectual life (although Bill Clinton has attacked tax breaks for foreign corporations and for runaway plants, the two most politically vulnerable corporate tax subsidies). Maybe what we need is a nationwide network of "Fair Tax Committees," like the network that worked so successfully to pass Proposition 13 in California, to push for some of these changes.

GREEN TAXES

A former French foreign minister, Jean-François Poncet, condescendingly remarked to an American journalist some time ago, "It's hard to take seriously that a nation has deep problems if they can be fixed with a fifty-cents-a-gallon gasoline tax."

He exaggerated, but not by much.

Here's what a dollar-a-gallon increase in taxes on motor fuels could accomplish:

- Raise $100 billion *every year* to invest in our own country. Most of those in favor of the tax advocate a gradual introduction to allow people to adjust, so the full savings would not be realized for five or ten years.
- Stimulate investments in alternative-fueled vehicles, which will certainly become a great global industry in the future. A higher gas tax, then, should help American industry become more competitive.
- Reduce gasoline consumption and auto emissions, thereby producing a healthier environment.
- Reduce our dependence upon Middle Eastern oil and the costly violence that dependency produces. It is usually assumed that a dollar-a-gallon tax would reduce gasoline consumption by about 18 percent, which translates into more than one million barrels of oil a day. Such a cutback could drastically reduce American oil imports

and make a serious dent in our balance-of-payments deficit.

A more direct way to reduce oil imports is an import fee; a levy of $5.00 per barrel would raise $55 billion over five years. This would obviously raise the price of gas, but the idea that oil from the Gulf is cheap is one of the greatest hoaxes ever perpetrated on the American public. By one calculation, the oil-related cost of defending the Gulf *before* the recent war was $14 billion for 1988 alone, which works out to $29.50 a barrel of additional crude-oil costs—paid by the U.S. taxpayer. And that does not count the cost of the war: in lives, in dollars, and in environmental destruction.

An increase of only fifty cents per gallon in the price of gasoline would generate $50 billion a year and still leave the price below $2.00, cheaper than anywhere in Europe or Japan. According to New York investment banker Felix Rohatyn, a fifty-cents-a-gallon increase would enable us to generate enough money to rebuild American infrastructure, create millions of new jobs, and reemploy many of the people who will be laid off as a result of defense cutbacks. Even a modest twelve-cent increase would raise $55 billion over five years, about the same revenue as a $5.00-per-barrel import fee.

But we're dreaming. Oil-import fees have too many enemies, particularly in the oil-consuming states of the Northeast. A dollar-a-gallon price increase is sheer fantasy, fifty cents is out of the question, and even twelve cents seems unattainable when you consider that Congress has voted down a gasoline tax increase of *five cents*. The key Congressional committees are dominated by the oil industry; as one Washington insider told me, "Before a member can get on the House Ways and Means Committee, he must first deposit his favorite child as collateral with the drillers and refiners."

Maybe someone could make a gas tax stick if he called it "the Persian Gulf Defense Tax."

U.S. environmentalists have come up with a number of other two-birds-with-one-stone taxes that would raise revenues by increasing the costs of pollution, resource waste, and other drags on the economy. Wouldn't it be smart to shift the tax burden from the "goods"—wages, savings, and investment—to the "bads"—all environmentally destructive activities?

GET THOSE CARS

• One bright idea is a "congestion" tax. Currently, an estimated 70 percent of rush-hour traffic is pure stop-and-go, wasting time, money, and fuel, and seriously contributing to air pollution. With a congestion tax, "smart cards" or electronic license plates linked to computers would record every car passing by invisible roadside toll stations. Drivers would then be billed, or their cards debited. Such monitoring devices are already in place in the United States in Dallas and San Diego, overseas in Oslo, and are planned in several more areas internationally.

World Resources Institute, an environmental research group in Washington, D.C., has calculated the effects of such a toll. If the congestion taxes were set just to reflect the costs of vehicular delay in terms of lost worker productivity, they would range from roughly $0.25 to $1.25 for a typical ten-mile urban trip. And traffic on the most crowded roads during rush hour would be cut back by about 7 percent.

That may sound like peanuts, but this little scheme,

if applied nationwide, would generate about $45 billion in taxes annually.

World Resources also calculated what we might expect if we *don't* find some way to reduce rush-hour traffic. In the past twenty years, vehicle miles traveled have increased by 90 percent, while urban highway capacity rose by only 4 percent. By the year 2000, just to keep traffic jams at today's level by increasing highway capacity, the cost of new construction would be about $50 billion— on top of the cost of repairing and maintaining existing roads.

▪ To complement a toll on rush-hour traffic, we could also purge the tax code of the provision that enables employers to provide free parking as an untaxed fringe benefit. Parking would be taxed as income, but employer subsidies for mass transit, car and van pools, buses, and the like could be tax-free.

▪ During the 1992 presidential campaign, Jerry Brown also talked about a "feebate," a fee on the price of every car that didn't achieve a certain mileage, with a portion of the money collected then rebated to every purchaser of a car that exceeds the mileage standard. The mileage threshold could be raised gradually every year.

In 1992, the state of Maryland passed the first such law, which mandated that come the 1993 model year, buyers of new low-mileage vehicles would pay a hundred-dollar surcharge, and buyers of fuel-efficient cars would receive a fifty-dollar rebate (the state would keep the profit). But shortly after passage, the federal government (specifically, the National Highway Traffic Safety Administration) ordered the state not to proceed with the law, which had mightily offended the politically powerful manufacturers of gas guzzlers. As of this writing, it isn't clear what Maryland's response will be.

▪ Another idea is a "pretend" tax increase called "Pay as You Drive" insurance. Motorists would pay at the pump for the 70 percent of their insurance that covers the cost of meeting claims, raising the *apparent* price of gasoline by fifty cents a gallon. Though this wouldn't raise any revenues, it *would* reduce the number of un-insured drivers and offer obvious environmental bene-fits.

A CARBON TAX

The Doberman of "green" taxes, the dream of many envi-ronmentalists, is a carbon tax, which would go straight for the jugular of the really dirty players, the industries responsible for global warming.

Carbon-dioxide emission is the largest contributor to global warming, and the United States is the world's largest single contributor of CO_2, in the form of fossil-fuel emissions, into the atmosphere. (Another major source of CO_2 is the destruction of forests.)

A carbon charge would be based on the carbon content of all fossil fuels: natural gas, gasoline, crude oil, and coal. The tax would be simple to administer: It could be levied at the earliest point in the production process, the wellhead, the minemouth, or, in the case of imported fuel, at the dockside. Legislation has been introduced in the House of Represen-tatives calling for a tax based on a Congressional Budget Office analysis of what it would take to stabilize U.S. emissions of CO_2 at current levels.

The legislation calls for a tax rising by the fifth year to $18.00 a ton on coal, $3.85 a barrel on oil, and $0.48 per cubic foot of natural gas. By the end of the five-year phase-in period, the tax would be generating an estimated $35 billion a year. That would be more than enough to help coal miners find new jobs.

NO SILVER BULLET

For a brief moment, Jerry Brown's flat tax captured imaginations as the elusive fiscal paragon: the perfectly fair, perfectly simple fill-it-out-on-a-postcard tax. Never mind that Brown messed up and delivered an idea that would both be stupendously regressive *and* cost the government $200 billion a year (on top of the $400 billion deficit).

Brown's proposal was based on a more carefully designed flat tax, developed in the mid-1980s by Robert Hall and Alvin Rabushka of the Hoover Institution at Stanford University, suggesting a single-rate flat tax on business revenues and wages.

The business tax, which would replace the corporate income tax, would be levied after subtracting the cost of all purchased inputs, including labor and new capital equipment. Thus, the tax would not discourage new investment. The combination of this tax and the flat payroll tax amounts to a uniform value-added tax that exempts only the return to new capital.

The problem with such a value-added tax is that it is regressive, because the rich spend much less of their income on goods than the rest of the population does. Goods would also become more expensive as companies passed on to consumers as much of the value-added tax as they could. The solution in Hall and Rabushka's proposal is to give each family a basic exemption and then tax wages above that level at the flat rate. They calculated that if each family had an exemption of $16,000 and the flat rate were set at 19 percent, the tax would generate as much revenue as the current federal income tax.

And we could all fill out our taxes during a coffee break. The working poor would keep their earnings, tax free. The exemption for investment would stimulate growth. There would be few economic distortions (i.e.: economic decisions primarily made to reduce taxes). And half the lawyers in the country and all the tax lobbyists in Washington would be looking for work—in itself, a powerful argument for the proposal.

It all sounds too good to be true, and it is. Here's what's wrong with the flat tax:

- It would increase taxes for middle-income people and lower them for the most wealthy. It would in no way restore the progressivity that the American tax structure has lost in the past decade.
- It doesn't allow deductions from federal income taxes for state and local taxes. Thus, it would make it much harder for revenue-starved localities to raise taxes. Cities would be hurt because taxpayers would be encouraged to move to lower-tax rural and suburban areas. By eliminating the tax exemption for interest on state and municipal bonds, state and local governments would have to pay more in debt service. More tax dollars would flow to Washington. And who wants that?

The flat tax is just one of several efforts to raise additional revenues without asking corporations or the wealthy to kick in more of a share. The current push for a "consumption" tax, similar to the European value-added tax, is the latest incarnation of this effort.

A consumption tax is the confiscation of choice of organized business interests, although a lot of smart individuals like it too. Regrettably, consumption taxes tend to fall heavily on the poor. To circumvent this, some people have suggested exempting some of the basic necessities of life—like food— and/or offsetting the consumption tax with a tax credit for the first $10,000 to $16,000 or so of income for a family of four. But now we're getting back into complications.

There are much better ways to raise revenues than by

building Washington a money machine that skims a percentage off every, or almost every, purchase that Americans make. Flat taxes and consumption taxes don't make much sense in a country with huge peaks and valleys of wealth.

CAPITAL GAINS AGAIN

The problem with the battle over capital gains (profits from the sale of assets like real estate and stocks) is that it has always been cast as a struggle of rich versus poor. Do you give capital gains favorable tax treatment, thereby coddling the rich, or do you tax returns on assets at the same rate as wages, thereby taxing all forms of income equally?

George Bush's proposal to lower capital gains, for example, gave breaks to profits from the sale of stocks and mansions and everything else imaginable. As a result, his approach would have given the wealthiest 1 percent of taxpayers 60 percent of the dollar gains. Not surprisingly, Congress said forget it.

On the other hand, Senator Tom Harkin (Dem.-Iowa) opposed *any* reduction of capital-gains taxes, on the grounds that the typical beneficiary would be "someone who bought stock at two-thirty in the afternoon, sold it at two-forty-five, and made a killing without making a product."

But all this class war misses the point: capital-gains taxes can be used both to discourage speculative behavior, the scourge of the 1980s, *and* to reward long-term investment and the risk-taking that produces jobs and new vehicles of economic growth.

The best way to do this is simply to have graduated capital-gains tax rates, based on the length of time that assets are held.

For example, you could tax profits made on assets held for less than a year at very high rates, of 50 percent or more—higher than the taxes paid on any other kind of income, and far higher than the current 28 percent capital-gains tax. Then you would stagger rates downward to very low rates of 10 percent or even down to zero on assets held for more than five or ten or more years (by which time inflation will have wiped out some of the gains anyway).

This scheme would penalize quick-buck artists and reward long-term-asset holders. To further encourage entrepreneurs you could give a preferential tax break to gains from an investment in a new, job-creating manufacturing business held for at least five years. This would reward risk, as capitalism is supposed to do, and steer investment to the chancy frontiers of technology, where the payoffs to society can be the greatest. Eccentric and driven people will always pursue their long-shot visions, whatever the tax rate. But if entrepreneurs could keep more of what they made, you might might encourage more normal people to bet their families by starting new high-tech businesses.

The revenue loss would be nominal, since start-up companies generate less than 1 percent of all capital gains. Yet among them are the industries of the future, and the countless job-creating businesses that most people depend on for their livelihood.

STAY-AT-HOME TAX DOLLARS

While researching this book, I came across a remarkable suggestion that was actually introduced as legislation in 1975 by Oregon's Republican senator Mark Hatfield. The idea was so radical that I called Senator Hatfield's office to find out what had been going on in his mind back in 1975. (In those days, the question would have been, "What was he smoking?")

The proposal was this:

Individuals could allocate up to 80 percent of their federal taxes to locally controlled neighborhood government organizations and take that sum as a tax credit (remember, that means straight off the top of their tax bill). The Feds would get whatever was left over.

Senator Hatfield's press secretary explained to me that the so-called Neighborhood Government Act had sprung from the imagination of a libertarian staffer now long gone. Senator Hatfield, I was assured, had not been fully aware of what was contained in the act introduced in his name. "He wouldn't support it now," the flack confided.

Too bad. What a concept! Spend your tax dollars at home! Now that we no longer have to confront international communism and have tired of secret government and imperial Washington and the twelve hundred government planes that do nothing but fly our public servants on their appointed rounds to the tune of $2 billion a year, it might just be time to stop writing Washington names on our checks.

Why not revive the senator's idea and allow everyone to allocate a modest percentage of their federal taxes—maybe 10 or 20 percent—to whatever approved nonprofit or local or national governmental organization they choose? Or allow a straight tax credit for nonsectarian charitable contributions, including donations to local or state governments and agencies, up to a certain limit of one's tax liability?

Existing state and local taxes would not be affected; we are talking about *federal* taxes only. Thus, the programs most affected would be those that are undertaken primarily or exclusively by the national government, like the military, the multibillion-dollar nuclear-weapons program, the runaway entitlement programs, the secret $30 billion (or so) intelligence network, farm subsidies, and so on.

Funny how the list includes all the programs that have gone madly out of control.

Legalistic killjoys argue that it's not constitutional to allow citizens to pick and choose where their tax money goes. That kind of freedom might tempt people to go overboard, like one New England couple did. For several years, Randy Kehler and Betsy Corner of Colrain, Massachusetts, filled out a Form 1040 and sent it to the IRS with a note explaining their conscientious objection to the government's overinvestment in standing armies and weapons building. They then gave away the exact amount of their tax liability to nonprofit organizations like their local homeless shelter, food bank, and veterans' outreach center. Obviously, the couple found that what their federal tax dollars *didn't* support was as upsetting as what their money *did* support. Unfortunately, their libertarian approach ended with the IRS seizing and occupying their house.

Now that the Cold War is over, however, this kind of citizen action may be picking up support. The U.S. Peace Tax Fund Bill, having been introduced (and ignored) in every session of Congress since 1972, finally had a congressional hearing last year. Conceived by a group of Quakers in Ann Arbor, Michigan, the bill would permit people conscientiously opposed to war to have that portion of their taxes destined for the military allocated instead to peacemaking, broadly defined. (More than 20 percent of federal spending is consumed by defense.)

The U.S. Peace Tax Fund bill would create a fund in the Department of the Treasury into which citizens who are conscientiously or religiously opposed to war could direct their federal taxes that would otherwise be given to the Pentagon.

The bill's sponsors in the House and Senate—including Mark Hatfield—note that conscientious objectors, who have been exempt from active combat for years, still have to support the military through tax paying. If it is a constitutionally protected right not to be forced into the military, the sponsors maintain, it should be a constitutionally protected right not to be forced to pay for war.

The U.S. Peace Tax Fund is the ultimate in taxation *with* representation. It gives citizens the power to claim a peace dividend: talk about a radical idea.

CUT SPENDING: STOPPING WASHINGTON'S CHECKS BEFORE IT'S TOO LATE

WE HAVE THE MEANS

Entitlements. The very word tells you what has happened: a proliferation of government benefit programs that are dispersed automatically every year, according to fixed formulas. No vote of Congress required. No hand of man. No give for the get. No-brainer.

These "rights"—to Social Security, Medicare, Medicaid, food stamps, veterans' pensions, et cetera—now eat up more than half the federal budget. They amount to a welfare state for almost everybody; a cornucopia of government handouts and tax breaks detached from any framework of need or fairness, economic efficiency or reality.

You'd be surprised what nice people you meet when you put a microscope to the welfare rolls. And you don't even need a microscope; all many of us would need is a mirror.

The solution is clean and simple and, up to now, politically impossible: *All government payments and tax breaks to individuals should be means tested*. Either we stop transferring scarce public resources to people who don't need them, or, at the very least, we make those transfers taxable. Period.

Poll after poll shows that most Americans favor limiting

government benefits, four fifths of which are not means tested. But until recently, no one even knew exactly who was getting the trillion dollars or so in federal entitlements. New data now show clearly that the wealthiest Americans collect *more* from the welfare state than the poorest do. Sixty years after the New Deal began, we have ended up with a broad swath of society that feeds off government just as hungrily as the old Communist party elites used to do in Eastern Europe. Like Poland and Russia and East Germany before us, we need to throw this burden off our economy.

Ponder these statistics:

- Civil service and military retirees with incomes over $100,000 collected $9.2 billion from the Treasury in 1991.
- On average, $50,000 in direct federal payments goes to each of the thirty thousand biggest-grossing farmers in America. That's $1.5 billion a year.
- Only one of every eight federal benefit dollars reaches Americans in poverty—most of the rest goes to the middle class, much of it for Social Security and medical payments.
- In 1991, households with incomes under $10,000 collected $5560 each, on average, in federal benefits, while households with incomes over $100,000 collected an average of $5690. Counting direct outlays and tax expenditures, or tax breaks that cost the Treasury money, the wealthier households pocketed $9280 and the poorer $5690.
- More than 60 percent of all federal benefits is spent on the 12 percent of Americans who are age sixty-five or older. In 1990, the United States spent $4500 apiece on its children, counting all local public-school funding, and $11,300 apiece on its elderly.

- The highest earners pay taxes on half their Social Security benefits. If people with household incomes of $62,000 or more paid taxes on all those benefits, we could raise $20 billion a year.
- The home-mortgage deduction, the government's largest housing-subsidy program, costs $37 billion annually. Eighty-one percent of that goes to households with incomes over $50,000, and virtually nothing goes to the thirty-six million people living in poverty.
- Medicare spends $19 billion a year on households earning more than $50,000.
- Tax-free employer-paid health care costs the Treasury $60 billion a year and benefits not one of the thirty-five million Americans with no health care at all or any of the thirty-two million people who pay for health care out of their own after-tax dollars.

A socialist economist, Rudolf Goldscheid, once noted, "The budget is the skeleton of the state stripped of all misleading ideologies." By that measure, the federal budget is exactly what you would expect from the best Congress money could buy.

Our ideological rhetoric, just like the Communists', thinly disguises a dense network of payments to the privileged.

While Ronald Reagan and George Bush were verbally shelling the welfare state, the flow of federal payments to the rich turned into a torrent. From 1980 to 1991, for example, the real value of government benefits received by households with incomes over $200,000 doubled—while average benefits going to those under $10,000 declined by 7 percent.

The cost of all present-day federal benefits is larger than the entire federal budget at the time that Ronald Reagan, the apostle of rugged individualism, rode into Washington.

■   ■   ■

The game can't go on, of course, because it is on a collision course with economic reality. In every decade since the 1930s, entitlement spending has grown faster than the economy. In the twenty-five years after 1966, according to the Heritage Foundation, entitlements metastasized by 1882 percent after adjusting for inflation, while GNP increased by 81 percent.

Today, federal entitlements, including tax benefits, consume more than 15 percent of GNP, a percentage expected to climb steadily through the 1990s. Not counting the $200 billion spent on tax subsidies, entitlements gobble up more than 45 percent of the federal budget.

What can we do?

First, we can realize that while these costs may be out of control, they are, contrary to the opinion of most business-as-usual sleepwalkers in Washington, definitely *controllable*.

Next, we need to lay down some rules of reform. The following were proposed by two authors—Neil Howe, a consultant for the Heritage Foundation, and Phillip Longman, a Florida journalist—who have studied and written extensively on the need for means testing:

1. Benefits should bear some relationship to need.
2. Since our major programs are universal, having a high income shouldn't disqualify someone from receiving *any* subsidies.
3. No one living near the poverty line should lose any benefits. The half of all households earning more than $30,000 a year—the median household income—should be the only half affected by any changes in the distribution of entitlements.
4. The quasi-contractual nature of at least some pro-

grams, like government pensions, has to be respected.

• • •

That leaves a lot of leeway. Here are some of the suggestions made by Howe and Longman for how means tests could be implemented and what the annual savings might be:

- For all cash and in-kind entitlements, withhold 7.5 percent of any benefits that cause total household income to exceed $30,000, and withhold an additional 5 percent at the margin for each additional $10,000 in income. The maximum reduction of benefits would be 85 percent for households with incomes of $190,000 or more. Total savings: $33.5 billion.
- Use the same formula to reduce military and civil-service pensions, up to a maximum reduction of 25 percent for households earning $70,000 or more. Savings: $7.6 billion.
- For all benefits conveyed through the tax code (like the home-mortgage deduction and the tax deductibility of employer-paid health insurance), set a limit on deductions equal to the average tax expenditure enjoyed by households earning $30,000 to $50,000; that is, nominally "middle-class" households. In 1991, this would have limited the total allowable mortgage-interest deduction to roughly $2500. Savings: $34.7 billion.
- Make Social Security taxable like any other cash income—excluding 15 percent of benefits, which would be an untouchable, untaxable entitlement to even the wealthiest of retirees. Also phase out half the tax exclusion on the insurance value of Medicare (net of Medicare

Part B premiums) for $30,000 to $50,000 households.
Savings: $16.9 billion.

Unlike many proposals to cut entitlements, like taxing all
Social Security benefits that exceed an individual's lifetime
contribution, the changes enumerated above would have reduced the federal budget by almost $93 billion in 1991, *without
touching the benefits of a single person in need.*

Nor do these suggestions exhaust the possibilities. George
Bush flirted once with the notion of doubling or tripling the
Medicare premium (currently $32 a month) for old people
with incomes over $100,000—before he dropped the idea.

We could, of course, quibble over where the means testing
of benefits should start. My own preference would be far below
$100,000 but higher than $30,000, a sum that enables many
families to hang on to barely middle-class status by their
fingernails.

What if we raised the means-test cutoff to $40,000, leaving
untouched all households earning less? No one has done those
specific calculations, but Neil Howe's guess is that it would cut
one fifth to one fourth of the potential $93 billion in savings.

That would still leave $70 billion to $75 billion in entitlements savings every year, enough to make a truly meaningful
reduction in the deficit.

Are these kinds of cuts remotely possible? Howe notes that
staffers at the White House Office of Management and Budget
told him that "ninety percent of the political indignation occurs on the first penny you cut. So why not go for the really
big bucks?" There's no avoiding the realization that the gravy
train must stop somewhere. Let's just make sure it stops short
of real pain and suffering.

THE 4 PERCENT SOLUTION

Another very simple proposal to shrink government spending would simply limit all expenditure increases to 4 percent annually—roughly, the average rate of inflation. This variation on the balanced-budget amendment would reestablish the dangerously severed connection between spending and economic growth.

The rule would put a single cap on all domestic spending, excluding net interest on the federal debt and the S&L costs (which should remain the only true untouchables in the budget—unless, that is, one longs for a complete financial panic and collapse). Thus, the 4 percent solution would get at the rising cost of entitlements, which were exempted from the automatic cuts leveled on excess spending by the Gramm-Rudman budget law.

Analysts at the Heritage Foundation, the conservative Washington-based think tank that came up with the 4 percent idea, figure that if their suggested cap had been initiated in fiscal year 1992, taxpayers would have saved $225 billion by 1995.

The 4 (or 3 or 5 or whatever the rate of inflation) percent solution would eliminate the current "fire walls" between domestic spending and defense spending, and between "entitlements" and "discretionary" domestic spending—arbitrary barriers that prevent one side's savings from being applied to the other. As long as they stayed within the overall limit, policymakers would be free to add to or eliminate any program. If there is no other way to do it, maybe this kind of formula would give politicians the guts to tackle the entitlement monster.

Across-the-board ceilings on spending, of course, still require politically painful choices on how to stay within limits. Let's assume, for example, that the rule would require limiting all cost-of-living adjustments on benefits, a frequently heard proposal. For a triple-dipping federal pensioner, that might mean a shorter stay in Bermuda. For a widow living on her Social Security, that might mean fewer meals.

Setting automatic limits on programs, in other words, still skirts all the questions of justice and equity and priorities that politics are supposed to decide. But in the absence of the wisdom, courage, independence, and open debate that are necessary to make politics work, formulas may be better than nothing.

A $70 BILLION DEFENSE BUDGET

The ultimate sacred cow—and one of the biggest wastes of taxpayers' money on the face of the earth—is the Pentagon budget. If we want to find the resources to do what we have to do to make the United States the envy of the world again, we don't have to look very far. The money is right there, being spent on your local military base, National Guard station, defense contractor, military research lab, and restricted-to-the-military golf course; that is, what isn't being spent on maintaining American troops overseas.

The president and Congress, terrified of the consequences of throwing people in uniform and in defense industries out into a lackluster economy, are treating the military budget like an enormous jobs program. As Leslie Gelb of *The New York Times* has pointed out, the Pentagon budget is now the biggest jobs bill in U.S. history, far bigger than Franklin Roosevelt's public-works program during the Depression.

As of this writing, we are going to spend *$1.5 trillion* over the next five years on weapons and warriors, a fortune that could otherwise be used to turn the United States into a bustling modern industrial powerhouse. This military pork barrel is distinctly not free enterprise; it is certainly not smart; and it is definitely not "defense," unless it is defense against political backlash.

Democratic congresswoman Pat Schroeder of Colorado explained it to me succinctly during an interview: "They used to talk about 'the threat' to justify gigantic levels of military spending. But now that 'the threat' is gone, it's become 'the jobs.' That's what that spending is all about now." Defense-related jobs account for less than 5 percent of the work force, but they have become the tail that wags the defense budget.

The inherent stupidity of the system is that military dollars buy fewer jobs than any other kind of federal government spending. We could be creating two or three times as much work by building roads and sewage systems. We could achieve immeasurably greater productivity by sending kids to college and to civilian training programs. We could build almost anything more useful than new submarines or fancy fighter planes or missiles. In terms of economic competitiveness, we are just shooting ourselves in both feet with all that military spending.

A couple of years ago, I anchored a television piece on waste in the military budget. I interviewed retired army general Ed Meyer, a former member of the Joint Chiefs of Staff, who told me that he could have gotten the same amount of defense with 25 percent less money if he had had to. There was that much waste in the army's budget.

That conversation came to mind when George Bush announced in 1991 that with the end of the Cold War, the dissolution of the Soviet army and navy, and the decision of the Eastern European nations to become capitalism's poor relations . . . the military budget would be reduced by 25 percent. But not, of course, before 1997.

Just exactly how much money could we save if we not only eliminated waste but scaled back to a *real* peacetime military? How much could we safely cut out of the defense budget and still be militarily protected? Were we any less safe in 1976, when we spent 203 billion 1990 dollars on defense—close to 100 billion dollars less than we are spending today, *with no visible enemies*?

Who has the best ideas about this critical, historic opportunity to turn our resources back to more realistic, rational, humane goals?

The outspoken but reluctant Ross Perot has said that time's up on America's defending Japan and Europe, and he's not alone in that sentiment. We are still spending *eight times* as much on defense as do Japan, Germany, Britain, or France combined—nations no less vulnerable than our own. We are burning through and shooting off *twice* as large a share of our national output as any of these other countries do—why and for what, no one in power can explain very well. That's $100 billion a year overspent right there. Half a trillion dollars over five years. Surely, the Pentagon is smart enough to figure out how to protect us with the trillion they would have left over after a sensible cutback.

A group of impressive authorities on defense aver that we could safely *halve* the military budget in five years. (That would free up roughly $150 billion a year, enough to pay for most —virtually all—the new initiatives suggested in this book and, if accompanied by means tests on entitlements and slightly higher taxes on the highest incomes, to retire the federal deficit as well.) One of those in this camp is William Colby, a former head of the CIA. In television spots for the Coalition for Democratic Values, a nonprofit group advocating greater domestic investment, and in speeches around the country, Colby has announced, "It's time to cut our military budget by fifty percent and to invest that money in our schools, our health care, and our economy."

A detailed recommendation to reduce the defense budget to $161 billion by 1998 has been put forward by senior analysts at the Brookings Institution. Their list of superfluous military hardware reads like a seven-year-old boy's Christmas wish list—only the boys who are getting these toys are considerably older and ought to know better. The B-2 bomber, the Midgetman ICBM, new generations of fighter aircraft and destroyers and submarines and warheads—all acquired or maintained while the former Soviet Union has cut military procurement and new-weapons development to almost zero, and Russian naval officers complain that they have become a coast guard.

We're still testing nuclear bombs in Nevada at a cost of almost $2 billion a year. We still have 395 military bases on foreign soil. We still shell out an estimated *$30 billion a year* for "intelligence," a budget so shrouded in secrecy that Congress, which holds the constitutional power of the purse, does not even know whether personnel cutbacks authorized for 1991 were even made—a definition of out-of-control if ever there was one. We do know, however, that billions are being spent on uncovering onetime Russian secrets that are now freely available to any television crew or potential investor.

And of course we must not forget our military mission in Europe, which includes schools, hospitals, commissaries, family centers, and housing for more than 200,000 *dependents* of the more than 200,000 troops still watching the Rhine. Unfortunately, Europe is too expensive now for most other American tourists. If you want to draw an analogy between the once privileged Communist party apparatchiks in Eastern Europe and the military beneficiaries of a fully socialized government support system, go ahead.

But Pentagon excess is to news what Mom is to Pop: old and familiar. Fresh excitement lies in imagining what's now possible in the new post–Cold War world—*a world in which the major military establishments are all on the same side.*

For the first time since the 1920s, we have before us the possibility of a truly cooperative international security system and a radical demilitarization of international affairs. With the collapse of the Soviet Union, we could implement a concept of national power based on economic strength and competitiveness, and a system of national security based on a world without offensive armaments.

If we summoned the imagination, the intelligence, and the guts to do it, we could immediately start building arrangements by which the most powerful nations could act together to protect weaker states from aggression, protect threatened peoples from genocide, and protect the beleaguered environment from annihilation. If we did that, we would really have won the Cold War. And we could enjoy a real victory dividend.

What do you think *that* kind of defense budget would cost? Would you believe $70 billion a year? That is how much a fully cooperative security policy might cost by the year 2000, according to Randall Forsberg, founder of the Institute for Defense and Disarmament Studies in Cambridge, Massachusetts. She figures that $70 billion would handily pay for a military posture based on minimum deterrence, nonoffensive defense, nonproliferation, and multilateral peacekeeping.

Together, the United States, Canada, the countries of Europe and the former Soviet Union, and Japan account for 85 percent of world military spending. To establish a cooperative security system, these countries would have to agree

- to replace their traditional armed forces with small "nonoffensive" defenses of national territory, including border guards, national guards, short-range coastal-defense boats, and short-range air-defense forces. They would eliminate large standing armies, long-range air forces, and oceangoing "blue water" navies.
- that the nations with nuclear forces could maintain small "minimum deterrent" forces, including submarines, until a fully cooperative security system was in place. Any further acquisition of nuclear, chemical, or

biological weapons or ballistic missiles would be outlawed.

- that for peacekeeping purposes, nations could also retain under their own command relatively small contingents of ground, air, and naval forces. These smaller forces would be highly mobile, cost-effective, lethal units, utilizing the latest technologies and munitions. Each major country might maintain a force about half the size of the combined Desert Storm forces; all together, the industrial nations might retain the equivalent of three or four times the Desert Storm forces. (Today, the former Cold War adversaries have a military strength of ten to twenty times the size of a Desert Storm–equivalent force, assuming that the former U.S.S.R. had the wherewithal to mobilize its weapons and equipment—which it does not.)

No one country would be able to undertake a Desert Storm–sized operation alone; an aggressive use of force by any one country could be opposed by the others acting in unison. Thus, the U.N. Security Council could respond to an act of aggression anywhere in the world, but no single nation would have the capability for large-scale unilateral military intervention.

One possible cooperative security model might differentiate among the roles played by various nations. Combat forces could be drawn in proportion to the population of each participating nation, while the United States and the former Soviet Union could provide the bulk of global surveillance, communications, transportation, and logistical support for the multilateral forces.

- that nations would use diplomatic and economic sanctions—and military action, if necessary—to stop nuclear, chemical, or biological weapons proliferation, to ban weapons exports, and to encourage regional arms reductions and the establishment of nonoffensive defenses in the rest of the world.

According to Randall Forsberg, the $70 billion a year that the United States would have to spend on such a scenario would include $5 billion to operate ten strategic submarines; $1 billion for the existing U.S. air-defense system; $1 billion for National Guard forces; $12.5 billion for global surveillance and communications; $14 billion for the same air-lift and sea-lift capability as exists today; and $34 billion for ground, air, and naval forces (about half the size envisaged by the Brookings Institution analysts who would cut the military budget in half.)

If all this is too utterly frightening, too close to love-beaded, pony-tailed pacifism, for another $16 billion the United States could retain three aircraft carriers, with one always quickly available in a crisis, plus one division of marines, a marine air wing, and amphibious assault ships to be used as support for multilateral peacekeeping efforts or even unilateral muscle flexing. This option would increase the annual U.S. military budget to only $86 billion a year.

Over the next five years, the United States could move toward this goal by implementing the recommendations to halve the defense budget, while simultaneously negotiating agreement on the purposes, organization, and command of multilateral peacekeeping forces. If a consensus is developed, the "New World Order" could be gradually established in subsequent years; we could be rolling in the money needed for domestic programs, and we would all be safer in our beds than we have been for fifty years.

Think of it as a choice between becoming an armadillo or a dinosaur. General James Gavin used to explain that the dinosaur is the more frightening, formidable beast, but that the armadillo is more flexible, more adaptable, and better protected from its enemies. Which one is still around today?

An opportunity like this will never come again in our lifetimes, if ever. Do we have the sense, the optimism, and the survival instincts to go for it?

· II ·

How to Invest a Victory Dividend

A NEW G.I. BILL

One of the most moving philanthropies of the past decade is the I Have a Dream Foundation, through which a wealthy patron "adopts" a class in a low-income grade school and offers a free college education to anyone in the class who ultimately qualifies. Knowing that the opportunity is theirs, many of these kids, defying all odds, do end up in college. The program proves that the talent is there, even in the poorest surroundings, and that given hope and a chance for bettering themselves, many ghetto youngsters can make it.

If you're like me, you may also find this a little sad—that we are still relying on nineteenth-century-style charity to give a tiny handful of kids a shot at climbing out of poverty. Why can't we offer the classic American dream of higher education to *every kid* who qualifies? We can, and in fact, almost fifty years ago we virtually did.

The historic Servicemen's Readjustment Act of 1944, widely known as the G.I. Bill, raised the educational level of an entire generation of men (95 percent of its beneficiaries) and made possible the great expansion of the middle class that followed the war years. If there was ever any question that investment in people is at least as essential as investment in plant and equipment, the G.I. Bill provided the answer.

Laid-off military and defense workers—many of whom lack a college education—need a new G.I. bill just as much as their World War II predecessors did. And *all* bright teenagers should be able to fulfill the dream of going to college—if they earn it with study and good grades, and are willing to pay back the country with national service or out of future earnings.

A few years ago, a ghetto teenager in Washington, D.C., said to a mayoral candidate, "We are supposed to say 'No' to drugs. But what are we supposed to say 'Yes' to?"

A new G.I. bill could answer that very tough question.

It would also be a boon to the millions of middle-class kids whose parents increasingly cannot afford the tuitions of prestigious universities—or of *any* university. During the eighties, college tuition costs exploded by about 40 percent in real terms, while the median family income rose by only 6 percent. At the same time, federal grants for higher education were largely converted into loans, so that those who try to stay in school are going more heavily into debt in order to pay for their education.

A survey taken *before* the recession found that one third of the students interviewed had delayed or indefinitely put off college because of the expense. At the nation's most acclaimed universities, the proportion of students from families earning more than $100,000 a year rose sharply during the 1980s.

Those who doubt that a renewed G.I. bill could do much to remedy these trends should remember that few people in the 1940s thought the idea was particularly promising in the first place. The original G.I. program offered tuition, fees, books, and a monthly stipend of $75 (equivalent to about $450 today) to any veteran who wanted to go back to school. The elite were not thrilled: Robert Hutchins of the University of Chicago predicted that idle vets would turn campuses into "hobo jungles," and James B. Conant of Harvard feared that academic standards would be undermined.

Initially, it was predicted that about 150,000 people would sign up.

In fact, almost half of all veterans—more than 7.8 million people—took advantage of the government's offer (counting college, precollege, and on-the-job or farm training). The overall $14 billion price tag was enormous; at the peak of the program, in 1949, the annual cost came to $2.7 billion—almost 1 percent of the GNP. But no one has yet been heard to say that it wasn't worth it. A recent Congressional study concluded that the additional taxes paid by the college-educated veterans during their working lives more than paid for the program.

What would a similar program cost today? One way to make it affordable would be to require the beneficiaries of a new G.I. bill to pay back the government either through deductions from future earnings or by two years of low-paying community service.

During the 1992 presidential campaign, Bill Clinton advocated scrapping the jerry-built $6 billion student-loan programs (by 1991, defaults and bank subsidies for student loans were costing the federal government more than $3.6 billion) and replacing them with what he called the National Service Trust Fund. Clinton estimated that a sweeping new program, offering tuition in return for two years of national service, would cost an additional $8 billion a year. Balance that sum against the gains to society from having the services of hundreds of thousands of new child-care workers, police, teachers, and health-care workers.

If you expand Clinton's proposal to include, as the original G.I. Bill did, technical training (courses leading to a technical or professional certification), the cost would of course be greater. But today's needs would be even better served. Many members of the armed forces could acquire the specialized training they had hoped to get in the military. And with a civilian training program in place, Congress would find it far easier to reduce the hundreds of thousands of military personnel.

It is difficult to put a figure on the cost of that kind of expanded G.I. bill, but the Commission on the Skills of the American Work Force estimated that a comprehensive school-to-work training program would cost roughly $36.2 billion a year more than is currently being spent on sixteen- to nineteen-year-olds. That cost would look far lower if you counted current military and criminal justice expenditures on that age group and factored in student-loan defaults.

There are several ideas on where to find that money, not counting the obvious place: the military budget.

- Individual Training Accounts (ITAs) could be established, providing students with an education stipend and a voucher good at an accredited institution. Such grants would be considered "withdrawals" from students' ITAs, and would have to be repaid upon subsequent employment. Equal contributions to ITAs, up to a fixed amount, could be required of employers, but the ITA would be tied to the worker, not to the job.

The ITA would be a lifetime account. If an individual lost his job, the funds in his ITA could be withdrawn, tax free, in the form of a voucher for retraining at a certified institution. A new job and a new employer would replenish the ITA again, up to a ceiling. At retirement, both worker and employer would be entitled to withdraw their contributions, along with tax-free accumulated interest.

The ITA, in short, would be a self-financing trust fund, giving people "occupational insurance," a new kind of social security, throughout their working lives. We have health and accident insurance, old-age and unemployment insurance, and subsidies to preserve jobs in dying industries. But with increasing job insecurity, we need insurance making it easier for working people, from their late teens through retirement age, to learn new skills and professions.

• Another ambitious "pay as you earn" idea has been dubbed the "Equity Investment in America Program." It would use part of the Social Security surplus to make loans to students for training, retraining, or higher education. These loans would have to be repaid within twenty-five years, and annual repayments would vary with the level of each borrower's income: If one's earnings declined or ceased, the repayment amount would automatically adjust; moreover, students would not feel pressured to go into high-earning professions in order to repay fixed short-term loans.

Repaid loans plus accrued interest would be returned to Social Security. According to calculations, if the program assisted about nine million students each year, its debt to the Social Security Trust Fund would grow over the next thirty years (during which time the fund's surplus is also expected to grow). Thereafter, repayments would begin to reduce the debt, which would be eliminated by the year 2039. After that, the EIA fund would provide a substantial return to Social Security at a time when the Social Security balance is scheduled to decline.

EIA's proponents argue that the scheme "provides for a level of intergenerational equity not available through any other device and furnishes the Social Security Trust Fund with an investment opportunity second to none"—an investment in a better-educated, more highly skilled, and wealthier work force.

However we finance it, universal higher education's time has come. This country has still not really celebrated winning the Cold War; what better victory present than this could we give ourselves?

CIVILIAN POLICE AND THE TEACHER CORPS

Many of the defense workers and military personnel who will be losing their jobs in the post–Cold War era are highly skilled technicians, engineers, and machinists. Don't they deserve better than a pink slip for a job well done? As Georgia's Democratic senator Sam Nunn has pointed out, "They are not losing their jobs because they failed—they are losing their jobs because they were successful." Why can't this enormous reserve of talent, energy, and expertise be part of the solution to our economic mess instead of part of the problem?

These trained individuals won't find civilian work as easily as their counterparts did after previous wars. Manufacturing jobs, for example, now make up only about 16 percent of all jobs in the United States, compared with 35 percent after the Korean War (and 32 percent in present-day Germany).

An imaginative idea on how to handle demobilization comes from lawyer Adam Walinsky, who argues that the federal government ought to keep the troops on its payroll and use them for three- or four-year stints of civilian service, as police or teachers. And why not, Walinsky suggests, assign medical corpsmen to hospital emergency rooms and public-health programs?

For some time, Albert Shanker, president of the American

Federation of Teachers, has said that the nation should enlist discharged servicemen to teach in primary and secondary schools and even in jails. We still have thirty-three thousand people in the military who do nothing but recruit. These people know how to reach and motivate young people. They know how to teach skills and how to deal with kids from impoverished backgrounds (many were themselves raised in inner-city ghettos), and they wouldn't be afraid to go into tough, violence-plagued city schools.

Some of our awesome problems of race and urban decay could be addressed by a transitional program that brought the troops home to be "inspiring examples to the legions of lost black and Hispanic children in ghettos across the country," as Adam Walinsky puts it. The military's experience with young people and the potential role models it has produced are a vast national resource that we shouldn't allow to fade away in the drive toward disarmament.

Senator Nunn has proposed allowing military personnel to leave the armed services after fifteen years and build up their retirement credits with five additional years of civilian police work, teaching, health care, or participation in other vital professions. "If we act wisely," he said, "we can turn the enormous problem of excess talent in defense occupations into the enormous asset of new talent in nondefense occupations."

Senator Nunn's idea might also aid in solving another crucial domestic problem, this one having to do with the police. Financially strapped cities have had to reduce the number of police on the streets, even though we know that the cop on the beat deters crime.

At the same time, the Los Angeles riots proved that a paramilitary police force doesn't work. Rambo law enforcement results in brutality and insensitivity to the needs of the community; the results are—were—predictable. The LAPD had earned so little prior goodwill in the rioting communities that when rioting began, the police turned tail and ran, leaving law-abiding people at the mercy of the mob.

To counteract the possibility that onetime servicemen might "militarize" the police, it would help to have a simultaneous inflow of a different type of new blood into law enforcement. Clinton's idea is to allow young people to perform two to four years of police work, preferably in their own towns and cities, in return for free college tuition. It has been estimated that such an ROTC-type "community police" program would cost $300 million in its first two years. That is approximately half the cost of two days' rioting in Los Angeles.

A RECONVERSION EXPERIENCE

In retrospect, bringing the troops home after World War II was a piece of cake compared with the difficulties in demobilizing the American economy today. The United States reduced military spending by 90 percent in the three years after 1945, despite economists' warnings that another depression would be the result. The economists were ignored and, of course, proven wrong.

Today, the situation is strangely reversed. Far from demanding a peacetime conversion, the public seems to have forgotten what peace is. Yet economists are telling us that military cutbacks are essential if we are to regain our economic competitiveness. Who will turn out to be right this time?

One thing seems certain. If we are going to have a peace dividend (Massachusetts Democrat Barney Frank prefers the term "victory dividend"—after all, he says, we won, didn't we?), we have to persuade all those who lived off the Cold War—the huge standing army and the National Guard, the defense contractors and their employees and supporting communities—that the end of the war is not the end of the world.

A few big, bold programs, like a new G.I. bill, a civilian

national service, an apprenticeship program, and an American Development Bank, or "National Capital Fund," to finance a massive public rebuilding program, would eliminate much of the problem. Investments in people, transportation, and new technologies can provide skills, jobs, and hope, and are far more productive than further investments in the military budget.

These aren't just assertions. Between 1961 and 1990, the Department of Defense converted almost one hundred bases to civilian use. More than 93,000 jobs were lost—with much accompanying weeping and wailing—but more than 158,000 new jobs were created by the civilian airlines, airfreight companies, industrial parks, and educational enterprises that moved into the former military facilities.

Professor Lawrence Klein, a Nobel Prize–winning economist at the University of Pennsylvania, found that spending cuts after the Vietnam War that eliminated 100,000 jobs in the short run ultimately created, through a more productive redirection of the money saved, more than 100,000 jobs to replace them.

Because of today's sluggish economy and the deterioration that has occurred in our infrastructure and manufacturing base, we will need far bolder programs than were called for after Vietnam. We need nothing less than a new economic agenda. Here are just a few of the ideas that have been discussed:

- As after World War II, the government could sell off surplus assets, including bases, at bargain prices.
- Tax laws could be amended to allow liberal credits of about 10 percent to all companies investing in new R&D and worker training, at least for a transition period.
- Pending a new G.I. bill, colleges and universities could follow the lead of Pace University in New York,

which offers half-priced tuition to onetime defense workers, and St. Louis Community College, which has worked
with the McDonnell Douglas Corporation to retrain and
find jobs for laid-off employees.

- Civilian employers could make a real effort to "hire
a soldier for peace." More than 100,000 men and women
will be leaving the military this year alone. Over 98 percent of them are high school graduates, and most possess
technical or other exploitable skills. Firms can obtain
more information from the Army Career and Alumni
Program by calling 1-800-445-2049 and can register with
the Employer Network Data Base.

A subject of heated debate—and one with the most pro-
found implications for the future of the economy—is how to
demilitarize the two thirds of the *$70 billion* federal budget
for research and development that goes for military uses. (In
contrast, Germany allocates less than 20 percent of governmental R&D expenditures to defense; Japan, less than 10
percent. The United States spends only 1.9 percent of gross
domestic product (GDP) on nondefense R&D; the Japanese
spend 3 percent. Nearly one third of all U.S. scientists and
engineers are employed in military work.

This debate is part of the argument over whether the U.S.
government ought to involve itself in "industrial policy," that
is, play an active role in determining what industries and technologies the country ought to be investing in. Those who
argue against using government funds to promote investment
ignore the fact that the government is *already* highly involved
in channeling capital into the military, real estate, and agri-
culture. If only a fraction of the $46 billion or so of public
money that is being spent on military R&D could be steered
into more productive industrial and commercial sectors, we
would have no more talk about lost jobs and the declining
American economy.

• The National Academy of Science and Engineering has proposed putting roughly 10 percent of the military R&D budget, $5 billion, into a quasi-public "Civilian Technology Corporation" that would invest in "precommercial" civilian technologies. The board of the CTC would be entirely independent of the government, and its investment decisions would be made exclusively on technical and economic considerations. Industrial firms would compete for financing (and share the costs) of projects of interest to them.

Already, new industries are being planned around existing resources in regions most affected by military cutbacks: mass transit and electric cars, in southern California; the use of hydrogen as an energy source, in Connecticut; biotechnology and commercial and industrial aviation, in St. Louis. Companies involved in such efforts could submit ideas for applied research to the CTC and compete for investments individually or in consortia. The public investment would be spread over a multitude of projects and technologies, like a venture capital fund, and the government would share in any commercial profits that resulted.

• Democratic senator Barbara A. Mikulski of Maryland has proposed an environmental version of DARPA, the Defense Advanced Research Projects Agency, which develops and demonstrates innovative technologies for the Defense Department. The new agency, EARPA—would participate in the development of advanced *environmental* technologies, which currently receive only 2 percent of all federal R&D funds.

Working with industry, EARPA could help develop, among other things, cars powered by solar fuel cells and hydrogen-cycle internal-combustion engines, just as Defense Department funds once pioneered developments in computers, semiconductors, and jet aircraft. If the United States can win the race to produce a "green car," the first "zero emission" vehicle, what might happen to jobs and profits and that $30 billion annual trade deficit in autos and auto parts between America and Japan? Surely, the promise of an environmentally safe car (and other environmental breakthroughs) should inspire the same kind of national effort that spurred the race into space between the United States and the Soviet Union more than thirty years ago.

Make no mistake: Environmental innovation will be the basis of the important industries of the future, and many ideas will require public-private partnerships to reach the commercial stage.

▪ A complementary proposal has been made for a new National Institutes for the Environment—modeled on the National Institutes of Health—to conduct basic research on such projects as pollution prevention, waste disposal, ecosystem restoration, and sustenance of resources.

NIE grants would be disbursed after peer review, bypassing political favoritism and the other problems inherent in government bureaucracy. And the money would flow to the country's best universities and researchers.

▪ Washington is pushing the empire of government-owned research laboratories to focus more on commercially relevant research and dual-use applications of defense R&D. (The Defense Department has sixty-six labs that employ sixty thousand people altogether and spend about $7 billion a year; the Energy Department has three labs for nuclear-weapons design that employ twenty-four thousand people and spend $4 billion a year.) As part of the new effort, the Energy Department is working with thirteen companies in a metals consortium to incorporate new high-performance alloys into products like jet engines. And four government contractors have worked for four years on the Millimeter and Microwave Integrated Circuit program for military radar and communications, developing technology that has proven applicable to civilian-transportation needs in automobile obstacle-avoidance radar systems, automatic toll-collection systems, and vehicle communications systems.

In other projects, from energy extraction to superconductivity to lithography, private companies could decide what technologies seem most promising and match federal funds with those of their own to develop new fields. If any of the ultimate products were commercially successful, the government would receive a share of the royalties.

Such joint projects between government labs and private industry are still minuscule as a percentage of government research expenditures, and are frankly problematic. Industrial-bureaucratic collaboration may be as promising as some of the Japanese government-industry consortia, or as difficult as the attempt to convert Soviet state factories into flourishing private companies. We'll find out.

▪ As for megascience projects like the manned exploration of Mars, the human genome, the superconducting supercollider, and the $40 billion space station, these now appear to be too big for any one nation to tackle alone. Bill Spencer, president of Sematech, a government-industry consortium in the semiconductor field, says, "These are things we ought to do as a planet. We don't have to be macho and do it ourselves anymore."

· III ·

How to
Rebuild
the Country

More than two hundred years ago, Adam Smith wrote that spending for public works and education was as important a function of the state as providing for the national defense and the maintenance of justice.

The inventor of the idea of free enterprise understood what markets could and couldn't do. Would that Smith's pale latter-day followers were so smart.

In our uncritical worship of capitalism, we have neglected both our public facilities and our people, and we need to make amends fast. Many of today's boldest economic ideas describe how we can channel new investments into both "public goods" and "human capital," and in so doing prepare ourselves for a more productive post–Cold War twenty-first-century world.

■ ■ ■

PUBLIC WORKS WORK

It is an article of economic faith that one of the things that got us out of the Great Depression was the public-works program. A whole alphabet soup of new agencies was born, from the C.C.C. (Civilian Conservation Corps), which put the unemployed to work planting trees and building roads in the national parks, to the W.P.A. (Works Progress Administration), which created beautiful and lasting works that still surprise us with their aesthetic daring. We see the fruits of this national endeavor all around us, from the great dams in the West to the stone fences along the Blue Ridge Parkway to the murals in Rockefeller Center.

Today, these feats of artists and engineers are lumped together under the heading "infrastructure." One wonders if we have been slow to launch a grand new program of public-works investment because of that uninspiring name. Who could imagine rallying support for "massive infrastructure," or winning votes with a cry of "Infrastructure now!"?

But ask anyone who's banged over potholes, or waited endlessly for a subway train, or worried about the quality of the water coming out of the tap whether we don't need more "infrastructure." Ask the public officials who can't figure out how to dispose of this country's trash. And especially don't forget to ask the twenty-three-year-old lawyer in Washington, D.C., who parked his new Miata convertible in an underground garage and came back to find it underwater from a broken sewer main that flooded streets in the commercial center of the nation's capital for a whole day. (Not to be confused with the flood that ate downtown Chicago.)

When Americans *are* asked to approve new bond proposals for infrastructure, they overwhelmingly vote yes—by an 80 percent approval rate between 1984 and 1989. Voters in Denver approved nine separate spending packages in 1989 and *another* $100 million in 1991 for libraries; as well as funds for a new airport. According to Denver city council members, their city survived the recession in good shape because of a willingness to spend for needed public facilities.

Nationally, however, we are not making those investments. Our investment in infrastructure slid from a peak of 3.2 percent of GNP in 1968 to 1.6 percent in 1988, a decline which probably has something to do with the drop in our productivity growth over the same period. Why did this downturn happen? And why, with millions of people out of work, with a huge military-industrial demobilization coming down the pike, with airports overcrowded, roads clogged, and sewers crumbling; why, with wonderful new developments like bullet trains and short-haul aircraft and "smart highways" and fiber-optics systems to link every home, laboratory, and classroom waiting in the wings; don't we put people to work on a sweeping new federal public-works program?

The reason usually given is the enormous federal budget deficit. We don't have any money to spend on public works, goes the argument. The government is broke. We starved it, and overworked it on the military and entitlements, and now we can't take on any "new initiatives."

Increasingly, economists are beginning to call this line of argument by its real name: self-defeating belt-tightening. They can point to convincing evidence that money spent on "public capital" is not like money spent on tax cuts and consumer goodies. It is an investment that can significantly stimulate private-sector productivity and growth.

The Bank for International Settlements reported in 1991 that "regions investing more in infrastructure tend to have higher output, productivity, and employment growth." The Bank's examples? Germany, which spends fifteen times more than we do as a percentage of output, and Japan, which spends twenty-three times more proportionately.

To the rest of us, this "discovery" of the economic importance of the trillions of dollars' worth of public goods sounds like common sense. To old hands and veterans of the battle against the Great Depression, it's more like the reinvention of the wheel. But in economic and public-policy circles, the new appreciation of public capital is a radical breakthrough after the worship of private enterprise that passed for economic debate in the 1980s.

What exactly does the new research show? David Aschauer, formerly with the Chicago Federal Reserve Bank, and Alicia Munnell, of the Federal Reserve Bank of Boston, have both found a strong relationship over time between the productivity of private capital and the stock of public capital. Consider our national infrastructure. Good highways, for example, enable goods to be delivered faster, with less wear and tear on trucks and lower labor costs per units delivered. Trucking companies earn a better rate of return and are more likely and able to invest in expansion.

Congested highways, on the other hand, cost money. According to the Department of Transportation, delays and extra fuel consumption caused by roadway congestion cost the country's thirty-nine largest metropolitan areas more than $34 billion in 1988. Anyone who has ever tried to get to work during rush hour in northern Virginia can testify to the lost productivity involved in a simple traffic jam.

Looking at the state level, Munnell found the same effect: states with more public capital, all else equal, had greater levels of private output; and public-capital investment stimulates private investment and creates jobs, not just in the public sector but in the private economy as well.

The answer to the question "Can we *afford* greater public investment?" ought to be another question: "Can we afford *not* to make such investments?" Such expenditure is one of the few things that we could do to stimulate the economy in the short run *and* improve our long-term productivity.

According to another theory, persuasively laid out in a report by the Jerome Levy Economics Institute of Bard College, the economy is in a long-term depression that is being contained only by the enormous federal budget and such safeguards as deposit insurance. This depression was brought on by overproduction in the *private* sector—too many office buildings, fast-food restaurants, and shopping centers. Until all this excess is absorbed (which could take the rest of the 1990s), new private investment will remain weak. The key to economic revival, then, is increased *public* investment, which could substitute for business-capital investments.

Peter Drucker, a professor of social sciences at the Claremont Graduate School in California, makes a similar argument. The big new markets of the future are not in consumer goods or producer goods, he asserts, but in infrastructure: communications, environmental equipment, transportation, and the like.

Unless we recognize that this is where the action has to be, the Levy report warns, "The economy will continue to perform dismally for much of the 1990s, perhaps for the entire decade."

If there is mounting agreement on the need for infrastructure investment, there is less agreement on how the necessary financing will be mobilized. Estimates of the annual cost of repairs to existing facilities alone range from the $113 billion posited by the Association of General Contractors (do you smell a pork barrel?) to the less self-interested $38 billion offered by the Congressional Budget Office. When the cost of *new* facilities is thrown in, one gets easily to the $500 billion to $1 trillion range over the next ten years.

(In 1991, Congress did pass a highway bill providing $151 billion over six years, a 50 percent increase in federal spending on surface transportation. To put that in perspective, Taiwan, less than one third the size of Pennsylvania, has announced a six-year, $600 billion plan of public-infrastructure investment. And the unified German government is investing $1 trillion in the former East Germany, a territory of 17 million people—fewer people than live in New York State.)

The money for rebuilding America need not and cannot all come straight out of overextended federal, state, and local budgets. A number of new financing mechanisms are ripe to be tried.

AN AMERICAN INVESTMENT BANK

One of the many great innovations in American foreign policy was the commitment to rebuild the countries devastated by the Second World War. As the Cold War deepened, this reconstruction effort extended to the promotion of non-Communist economic development throughout the Third World, a mission that soon dominated the new International Bank for Reconstruction and Development, or World Bank.

Now that the Cold War is over, we can pay more attention to the parts of our own country that increasingly resemble the underdeveloped regions of the world. New York City, Los Angeles, Chicago, and Washington all have their potholed streets, burned-out neighborhoods, decaying water mains, and idle, wasted youth. Parts of the South and Southwest rival Latin America in their backwardness and shameful infant mortality rates.

Why don't we tackle these conditions with an American Investment Bank, modeled after the World Bank? What about a financial institution that could provide financing for infrastructure and urban and rural development in our own country?

Like a domestic equivalent of the World Bank, an American Investment Bank could fund long-term economic development projects. As proposed by Jesse Jackson during the 1988 presidential campaign, the AIB would be capitalized with pledges from state and municipal governments, although only a fraction of the money would have to be "paid in." That subscribed capital, and dedicated tax revenues, would serve to back bonds sold on the open market.

Using a similar structure, the World Bank has become the bluest of blue-chip investments, able to raise six dollars for every one dollar put up by its member nations. Maybe a strictly U.S. bank wouldn't be able to achieve that kind of leverage, but a three-to-one "gearing ratio" might be plausible. The AIB would invest its capital on projects screened and developed by its staff in conjunction with local governments, other major bondholders, and (if I were designing the thing) local environmentalists.

Washington wouldn't have to enter the picture except perhaps to encourage this new form of federalism by giving the bank a strong foundation with its own capital contribution. If there were a federal contribution, Washington's representatives would hold proportional seats on the board. The AIB would remain, however, principally a vehicle of the states themselves.

Some individual states already have their own development banks, but a national AIB would enable states to combine their capital and human resources on major infrastructure projects. Projects in one region could use R&D and suppliers from other regions, and competition to set up high-tech research centers could be avoided. And unlike a public-works program administered in Washington, the AIB would ensure that project priorities and decisions would be made by those most closely affected.

LET PRIVATE MONEY PAVE THE WAY

No government in the world today—federal, state, or local, German or Japanese—is solvent enough to pay for all the infrastructure it needs. To do the job, we will have to tap private capital.

Professor Peter Drucker argues that much new infrastructure can be built and operated by profit-seeking enterprises operating with funds from institutional investors. His organizational model is the private investor-owned utility, invented in the United States in the second half of the nineteenth century and subsequently used to build railroads, telephone companies, and power plants.

The private financing of infrastructure that is already taking place nowadays, however, looks more like the old canal and turnpike companies of the early 1800s. In California, four highway projects are being built by private interests; in one of them, a private consortium has contracted to build, finance, and operate a toll road in San Diego, in return for a thirty-five-year franchise to keep all monies collected. Ownership would subsequently be turned over to the state (just in time for major repairs, no doubt). A private company in Virginia is planning a similar project to extend a toll road from Dulles Airport to Leesburg, Virginia.

The problem with such projects is that they depend on user fees to pay back the original investors, and not all (or even most) infrastructure projects can charge enough to attract sufficient initial private capital. A more mixed public-private partnership model is probably called for, to wit:

- Projects could be financed by bonds issued by states, cities, and other public enterprises. The private sector could finance, say, 20 percent of a project at market rates, and the Treasury could buy 80 percent of the paper at below-market rates. The difference between what the Treasury pays for money and what it earns on the bonds would be the subsidy to the project. The cost to taxpayers could be spread out over the life of the project, rather than taken as an expense all at once.

The issuers could service the bonds with revenues from user fees—or perhaps from higher gasoline taxes—and the loans would be limited to levels that those revenues could support. This blend of public-private finance would leverage taxpayers' money and probably bring discipline to the public-works program. The presence of private investors would help prevent projects from becoming costly boondoggles.

• Or the Treasury could invest part of the Social Security Trust Fund surplus in high-grade state and local infrastructure bonds. At the moment, the surplus, which is accumulating at the rate of $1 billion a month, is being invested in U.S. Treasury long bonds. In other words, the fund is financing the federal budget deficit, going into long-term IOUs to a profligate debtor who shows no signs of curbing his appetite for nonproductive consumption.

Arguably, that Social Security money would be more productively spent on state and local infrastructure bonds backed by a federal guarantee. A proposal to that effect has been introduced by Democratic congressman Robert Matsui of California and Democratic senator Bob Graham of Florida.

NO MORE HIPPIE ACCOUNTING

Before we can begin to reinvest in America, we need to change the way the government keeps its books. Unlike corporate accounting, federal budgetary accounting makes no distinction between current expenses and productive investments.

A new communications system is treated just like a welfare payment or interest on the debt. *Anything* that is financed through borrowing is treated as if it were deficit spending, which makes about as much sense as saying that a person who borrows $200,000 to buy a house is $200,000 poorer. Or that a company that spends a million dollars on new equipment is no better off than a competitor that gives its CEO a million-dollar bonus.

Many of the nation's officeholders want to put government spending on a more businesslike basis. The federal government's investments in infrastructure could be put into a national capital budget, which would permit us to lay out a national long-term investment strategy. We could weigh the need for investment in public facilities against the need for investment in defense programs, and distinguish long-term capital investments in domestic civil works from short-term federal operating expenditures.

Such a budget could consist of these basic components:

- an inventory of the nation's public facilities, coupled with an assessment of their physical condition
- an estimate of additional capital-investment needs, which would form the basis for generating political support for whatever improvements and additions are needed
- an estimate of operating and maintenance requirements
- the identification of sources of financing
- the allocation of responsibilities among the various levels of government and between the public and private sectors.

Looking at what a capital budget could do, the obvious question is: How do we operate without one? The answer: We don't very well—this is one of the main reasons our infrastructure has deteriorated.

Another way to cut the federal budgetary pie is to divide it into three parts: past, present, and future. The past budget would include interest payments on the national debt and the costs of rescuing S&L depositors. The present budget would include current spending on the military and Social Security. The future budget would include investments in infrastructure, education, and research. Bill Clinton proposed this, and was accused of trying to find a way to call all social spending "investment."

But slicing federal spending in this fashion reveals that the government of the United States is spending only 9 percent of its budget on the future. Many economists believe that that share ought to be doubled, at least.

THE PEOPLE'S MONEY

One economic challenge faced by the country is how to utilize the savings of American working men and women to create jobs and promote economic growth. How can we ensure that at least some of the roughly $3 trillion dollars salted away in pension funds provides capital for long-term, growth-oriented investment?

This question has become even more pressing as the nation's intrastructure has deteriorated. With public budgets at all levels dangerously in the red, many observers are asking how pension funds can provide some of the needed capital.

The issue has also moved to the fore because of the sheer size of the country's pension funds. Even though fewer and fewer workers have private pensions, those who do saw the value of their savings soar during the 1980s, thanks to the rise in the stock market. This growth parallels the decline in the importance of commercial banks and S&Ls. Pension funds constitute the largest untaxed pool of capital in America, and we can expect a louder and louder debate about who controls that capital and how it is to be invested.

Pension funds' share of total financial assets has grown from 15 percent in 1966 to almost 26 percent in 1989. In 1990, total assets were $2.9 trillion, *more* than the current value of common shares trading in the stock market ($2.7 trillion in 1990) and almost equal to all the assets in the banking system ($3.2 trillion in 1989).

Pension funds' unique long-term liability structure (that is, owners can't get the money until they retire) should enable them to invest in long-term, productivity-enhancing projects. When the first funds were set up, they were exempted from capital-gains taxes precisely because they were expected to be "patient" capital, invested for the long haul in American enterprise.

But that isn't how it's worked out. By and large, the funds, professionally managed, intermingled with and indistinguishable from all the other dollars out there, have played the game like everybody else, showering money on the Fortune 500, making scattered short-term investments, and chasing high returns anywhere and everywhere they seem to beckon.

Pension funds have been used to finance leveraged buyouts, dabble in speculative foreign real estate, and build one too many shopping malls. Despite some well-publicized mistakes, all this has earned the public pension funds in particular, and their millions of beneficiaries, healthy rates of return. Between 1980 and 1989, their assets grew by 267 percent. But one has to ask whether at least some of the money might not have been spent more productively, to help fill the very real gaps in the private-capital markets.

The public pension funds are in fact moving in this direction, toward what is now called "economically targeted investing." This is what used to be called "social investing"—putting private money to work, at market rates of return, in publicly useful projects.

A survey financed by the Ford Foundation found that in 1989, more than half the large public pension funds, especially state funds, maintained economically targeted investment programs into which they had collectively contributed some $7 billion. In the next two years, New York City public pension funds doubled their investments in affordable housing, small business loans, and the like to $850 million. The California Public Employees Retirement System, the largest pension fund in the state, voted in 1992 to invest up to $375 million in single-family houses, a move expected to create new jobs in California's sagging construction industry, increase the supply of moderately priced housing, and generate returns of more than 20 percent for the fund. In Pennsylvania, public funds have financed home mortgages at favorable rates, deposited money in banks that lend to companies that create jobs, and bankrolled student loans.

Some of the funds have come up with wonderfully imaginative ways to leverage their money. In one approach, a pension fund promises to purchase securities from Fannie Mae, the federal mortgage agency, that are backed by nonconforming mortgages (mortgages that don't meet the agency's usual restrictions). Fannie Mae, in turn, promises a bank that if it makes those loans, it can get them off its books by selling them to Fannie Mae. The effect: to broaden the secondary mortgage market and get housing loans to people who might not otherwise qualify.

Massachusetts, for example, introduced in early 1992 a program for "the forgotten middle class" under which twenty-nine banks and lending companies will offer mortgages to resident prospective home buyers; a state teachers' and employees' pension fund is providing $125 million to purchase securities from Fannie Mae that are backed by those mortgages.

The mortgages will offer relaxed qualification rules for anyone with an income of less than $68,000, and down payments will be as small as 5 percent of the loan. As an extra sweetener, the state employees whose savings are financing the scheme may be able to make down payments of as little as 3 percent. When this program was announced, Fannie Mae's switchboard was knocked out by seventeen thousand phone calls in one day.

Such investing can be profitable: The New York City Employees Retirement System says that its targeted investment program yielded an average return of 13 percent over the last five years, compared with 12.1 percent for the overall portfolio, as fund managers strove for "market rates of return" equivalent to returns on equally risky ventures, on their targeted investments.

Inevitably, though, there have been some big losers. Funds seem to make big mistakes when they put money into local companies in order to save jobs. A Connecticut investment of $25 million in Colt Industries doesn't look smart with the decline in military sales, and the public pension fund in Kansas lost $65 million in a failed S&L.

One could argue that these mistakes are no worse than purportedly prudent investments made in the 1980s. Pension funds suffered an estimated $38 billion in unrealized losses in the stock-market crash of October 1987. They have been taken to the cleaners in oil and gas deals, and, most recently, in real estate. In 1991, the value of the pension funds' billions of dollars invested in professionally managed property funds was written down by more than 25 percent, thanks to the plunge in the value of commercial real estate. Feckless American funds even dropped a bundle in the London property market. In light of all this "prudence," many state and local officials have reckoned that their employee funds might have done better being carefully invested in their own communities.

The broader point, probably, is that funds are best managed when they are invested for the long haul and are inclusive, or well diversified, like any other smart investment. The advantages of long-term diversification may be one of the major selling points for economically targeted investments.

One argument often heard against targeted investments is that if they were so great, the market would have already discovered them; in other words, "capital gaps" don't exist. Carol O'Cleireacain, New York City finance commissioner, tells this story in rebuttal:

When the New York City Police Fund set out to invest in small local businesses, its managers decided to buy securities backed by Small Business Administration loans, only to discover that the banks in the financial capital of the world were not making SBA loans. The staff of the fund's trustees actually had to bring in SBA experts to tutor New York banks. Now some large banks are making SBA-guaranteed small-enterprise loans, and the police fund is committed to investing $50 million in securities backed by the loans.

The point: Nothing, including markets, is perfect.

Let's pretend that Congress didn't spend a nickel, or hire one new bureaucrat, but merely passed a law saying that 1 percent of pension-fund assets had to be invested in public infrastructure and low- to moderate-income housing. The money would go into a "National Capital Fund" to meet long-term domestic needs. We're talking about $30 billion to start with, and up to $500 billion over ten years.

For the infrastructure investments, the fund could buy special state bonds that could be serviced through a portion of a national gasoline tax, an idea put forward by Felix Rohatyn. Bonds and securities issued by the federal secondary-mortgage agencies and backed by mortgages on affordable housing would also carry high investment-grade ratings and fully meet the fiduciary requirements of pension-fund trustees.

Those who think that this is an unimaginably radical proposal should know that New York City's largest retirement system already has a policy of investing as much as 4 percent of its assets in investments targeted to the city, and that Connecticut plans to invest as much as $300 million, or 3 percent of its state pension-fund assets, in Connecticut-based enterprises.

During the 1988 presidential campaign, Jesse Jackson called on public funds to invest 10 percent of their assets voluntarily in new federally guaranteed securities to finance small-business loans, low-income housing, neighborhood revitalization, and infrastructure.

This isn't a wild and crazy idea, like abolishing private property or asking children to pick up garbage (an idea dreamed up by a nineteenth-century utopian socialist who observed that kids loved playing with mud and getting dirty); compared to some of the other piquant visions of the truly radical, this is milk pudding. It is a proposal that is not going to go away.

Jesse Jackson raised the pension-fund issue in 1988. Felix Rohatyn raised it again in 1992, suggesting, in effect, a national economically targeted investment plan. The idea has taken root in the Democratic party (as of this writing, House Majority Leader Richard A. Gephardt's staff was preparing legislation, based on Rohatyn's concept, for a $500 billion, ten-year investment program in infrastructure, using federal revenues as backing for investment-grade bonds to be sold to public and private pension funds and other institutions).

By mid-1992, the only people who hadn't looked into this great idea were the Republican president and Treasury Department. But with new national leadership, pension-fund-financed investment will be off and running.

· IV ·

Health Care: The Best Solutions

HOW TO TELL THE REAL REFORM FROM THE PHONIES

You could say that our inadequate health-care system is an artifact of our almost century-long crusade against communism. Since the Progressive Era, back in the 1910s, American reformers have been calling for decent medical care for all. And since the Bolshevik Revolution of 1917, all its opponents have had to do to kill the idea is to scream "socialized medicine," with its dread images of concrete-block clinics and Stalinist surgeons wielding scalpels.

So maybe it wasn't an accident that the idea of universal health care came back to life as the Cold War died. The debate should be more interesting this time around.

A more proximate cause of the renewed debate, of course, is the utter failure of our current system to provide decent medical care at a reasonable price. Everyone knows it, and everyone is worried about it. According to polls, health ranked second only to the economy as the major election issue in 1992.

And why shouldn't it be? Some 35.4 million Americans, including more than 8.5 million children, have no health insurance at all (10 million additional kids have insurance only because of Medicaid). Tens of millions more are just one job, one spouse, or one bad accident away from medical indigence.

Americans who have medical coverage pay more for it, in premiums and copayments, than people anywhere else in the industrialized world. The United States has the distinction of being the only industrialized country except South Africa that has no limits on the cost of health care and that does not guarantee to its citizens affordable health-care coverage. This does not make for sound sleep at night.

People seem to realize that the time for fundamental reform is at hand. In a 1992 Harris poll, three fourths of those asked said that they wanted the government to set prices for health premiums, prescription drugs, and doctors' and hospitals' charges. Eighty-two percent expressed concern over their own future coverage. And the fraction of the American population dissatisfied with its health care had doubled in five years to more than 25 percent.

But that doesn't mean that fundamental changes will occur. The giant medical-industrial complex still calls the political shots, and neither major political party stands behind a coherent plan to give the people what they clearly want— universal coverage with strong controls on costs. PACs associated with the health industry now number more than two hundred, or two for every senator. According to a study released in 1991 by Common Cause, health PACs have given more than $40 million to members of Congress.

No group is more aggressive than the health-insurance industry, whose annual take is $35 billion to $40 billion a year. During conventions of health-insurance salesmen—held, conveniently, in Washington—literally hundreds of agent-lobbyists swarm over Capitol Hill, bad-mouthing basic reform; lawmakers admit candidly that the heavy pressure works.

It is no mystery why the United States spends more per person on health care than *any* other country or why health costs are rising faster than a Stealth bomber. Too much of the money that flows to doctors, hospitals, and insurers flows right back into the political system that put it there in the first place. The same money also makes sure that any fundamental national health-care reform that ever gets close to a vote is a victim of crib death.

Yet even these special interests can read the writing on the wall; and now everybody, from business to labor to health organizations, is for "universal health insurance." Even the American Medical Association, which has battled every effort to reform the system since 1919, supports a tighter health safety net. "It is no longer acceptable morally, ethically or economically for so many of our people to be medically uninsured," declared an editorial in the May 1991 *Journal of the American Medical Association*.

A cynical view of this kind of conversion was taken by Brad Lint, a Maryland staff member of Citizen Action. The industry "favors making taxpayers pay for the sick and the uninsurable," he told a reporter, allowing insurance companies to do a healthy business "covering the rest."

In this climate, it is important to know how to tell the difference between a real reform and a phony, proposed only to pacify all the angry people around the country and to let business continue as usual. But business *can't* continue as usual. The system is just too bankrupt, economically and ethically, as even the AMA says.

The Commerce Department estimated that we spent $817 billion on health care in 1992, an unhealthy 14 percent of the GNP. Back in 1965, the height of our postwar heyday, we were spending a mere 5.9 percent of GNP on health care. And all that money buys us an average life expectancy (seventy-five years for North Americans) that is not much longer than life expectancy in the extremely poor countries of China (seventy years) or Sri Lanka (seventy-one years).

The chief economist of the World Bank, Lawrence Summers, has observed that "a child born in Shanghai is more likely to become literate, more likely to graduate from high school, and more likely to live to be seventy-five than a child born in New York City."

In his January 1990 State of the Union Message, President Bush declared that he was "committed to bring the staggering costs of health care under control." In the next two years, costs rose another 16.6 percent compared with an 8.2 percent rise for the overall Consumer Price Index.

When I go to the superb doctor of my choice, I merely have to wait in the reception room for an hour or so and then share my appointment time with two or three other half-naked patients, all of us secured in our little cubicles as the harried doc dashes from one to the other in an efficient, market-oriented, time-managed frenzy. And then there are the forms, and the two-hundred-dollar charge for a routine fifteen-minute visit to the pediatrician, and the drugs the doctor is selling out of his own office.

But that is nothing compared to the lot of the estimated thirty-seven million people with no health insurance at all. If you are poor, your lack of coverage could be fatal, as is indicated by higher death rates that correlate with income, race, and lack of coverage.

As for business, the average company spends an amount equal to *45 percent of after-tax profits* (the equivalent of 12 percent of total payroll costs) on providing health-care coverage to its employees. The burden on business has grown so heavy that some companies even refuse to hire smokers, citing their higher medical bills. Increasingly, companies are winning the right to cut back on their insurance coverage to people with *any* indication of a chronic problem, including alcoholism, mental-health ailments, or a child with a birth defect.

No wonder virtually everyone agrees there has to be a better way. But which way do we go? By mid-1992, there had been at least thirty health-care bills introduced in Congress, a barrage of proposals so complex and confusing that it would task an expert to sort them all out. But if you strip away all the tinkering and the trivial "fixes," there are two basic approaches that stand the best chance of becoming the basis of a new medical system.

MANAGED COMPETITION

Under this scheme, individuals would be organized into large groups or health-maintenance organizations—through work, if they are employed—and represented by a sophisticated buyer, called a "sponsor," who would negotiate with hospitals and doctors for the lowest-cost treatment. Providers would be paid a fixed fee for each patient, independent of how much care he or she turned out to need—the same method health-maintenance organizations use to control costs. Incentives would be arranged so that all employers would have to join the system, and all consumers would have to opt into the least costly health plan chosen by their employer. (If you wanted a different plan, you would have to pay the entire cost difference out of after-tax income.)

The idea requires two changes in federal tax law. Currently, employer-paid health-insurance premiums are fully deductible, no matter how wasteful. There would have to be a cap on the deductibility of premiums to provide an incentive to seek low-cost managed-care plans. Second, small employers that refused to join large groups to buy medical insurance would be denied tax deductibility. Currently, small employers going it alone have an incentive to discriminate against job applicants with potential health problems.

The government would offer a plan for everyone who is self-employed or unemployed, which could be paid for in part with the tax revenues generated by limiting tax-free employer contributions. The Medicare program would evolve from its current fee-for-service approach and be contracted out by the government to health-maintenance organizations like those used by employers.

This approach was devised by the Jackson Hole Group, a group of health-care specialists led by Dr. Paul Ellwood, a physician and health planner in Minneapolis, Minnesota, and Alain Enthoven of Stanford University, formerly an official at the Department of Defense who developed a cost-benefit analysis used to justify the Vietnam War. The Jackson Hole Group asserts that once everyone is tucked into these managed-care programs, limits could be set on payments to the organizations and costs would be further reduced. This seems logical, though critics point out that such a plan has never been tried anywhere in the world.

In the real world, what has emerged is a bill, supported by about sixty conservative Democrats, mandating some of the basic ingredients of managed competition, including turning Medicaid into a managed-care program for every uninsured American.

But the legislation doesn't touch the sacred cow, Medicare, with its runaway costs; nor does it set any direct limits on overall medical costs. It simply contains a set of "incentives" to push employers and consumers into low-cost health-maintenance organizations. In the view of one critic, Stephanie Woolhandler of the Center for National Health Program Studies at Harvard University, "The managed-competition approach is basically a takeover of health care by the insurance industry."

Managed competition would certainly increase the role of the industry. Insurance companies would own and operate most of the managed-care programs and would parcel out the money to pay for the care of their members. The Health Insurance Association of America thinks this is a great idea.

The architects of managed competition deny that their intent is to throw federal support to the insurance companies in the Great Health Care Battle of the 1990s. But they are quite up-front about their intention to reform the current employment-based health-care system while rocking as few boats as possible.

As the Jackson Hole Group explained in one of its policy documents, "Seeking politically feasible incremental change, [we propose] to build on that system and correct its deficiencies rather than replace it radically."

ONE INSURER

The other realistic alternative to the current system is not so solicitous of the powerful insurance companies; rather, it would put them out of the health-insurance business altogether. That is precisely what makes the plan so cost-effective. The idea is to establish a single insurer: the federal government.

A new national-health scheme could be modeled on the Canadian system, which works exceedingly well at a fraction of the cost of American medicine. Essentially, taxpayers would finance health coverage for everyone. All Americans would receive government-paid, privately-delivered hospital, doctor, and dental care, as well as prescription drugs, mental-health services, and long-term care. No one would ever see a medical bill, and all citizens could choose their own doctor, hospital, or nursing home. The government would regulate fees and budgets to keep costs within bounds.

The system would be financed by increases in taxes on the

top 5 percent of taxpayers, rising to a 38 percent top bracket on those earning more than $200,000 a year. Illinois Democratic congressman Marty Russo, who was the chief sponsor of the leading national health-insurance bill before he lost a reelection bid in 1992, contends that having a single insurer would save $67 billion a year in administrative expenses. If all that money were used for health care, along with the additional tax revenues, the government would still save $3 billion a year, and 95 percent of Americans would be spending less for health care than they spend today. Businesses wouldn't have to buy health insurance for employees; consumers wouldn't have to pay insurance premiums or deductibles; hospitals wouldn't have to raise fees to cover bad debts.

The key to the greater economic efficiency of the Canadian approach is its simplicity. One insurer means far lower nonmedical expenses. In Canada, billing and administrative paperwork adds up to only eleven cents of every dollar spent on health, compared to twenty-four cents of every health dollar spent in the United States. Insurance overhead in Canada is 1 percent of health costs, versus 10 percent in this country. (Medicaid and Medicare spend 2 to 3 percent of the money they take in on administration; for-profit insurers keep 12 to 14 percent of revenues, less than 1 percent of which goes for taxes.)

Republican critics claim that so many people now uncovered would seek care that a Canadian-style system would raise costs by tens of millions of dollars a year (even if this is true, at least the money would be spent on *care*, not on wasteful administration). But support for a single-payer system is building among congressional Democrats—House Majority Leader Richard A. Gephardt has endorsed it, as have such influential members as John Dingell of Michigan, and Henry Waxman and Pete Stark of California. The Russo bill has more sponsors than any other piece of medical legislation in Congress, but guess who is violently opposed to it? The powerful private-insurance companies. Medical reform of this type has no chance unless a president gets behind it.

PLAY OR PAY

Much has also been written about "play or pay," a dual system of public-private insurance. Employers would have to provide employees with a private package of core benefits or pay a tax equal to about 7 percent of payroll into a public fund that would finance coverage for the uninsured. This is the preferred solution of the big industrial companies and their unions, the AMA, many hospital groups, and many congressional Democrats as well.

Critics, however, insist that play-or-pay is a nonstarter. For one thing, it could raise costs by tens of billions of dollars a year. Small businesses, many of whom offer no health insurance at all to their employees, claim that play-or-pay will be their financial ruin, forcing them to cut payrolls.

But if the tax rate is set low enough to satisfy such hard-pressed businesses, other employers who now offer insurance could drop it and simply pay the tax. Eventually, that could push most people into a national health system.

Whichever way Congress decides to go, strict cost controls are going to be essential, for any scheme to get care to all Americans is going to be expensive. Some health economists say that universal insurance could drive up costs by as much as $50 billion every year. *Only if we control costs can we have universal health care without increasing taxes on most Americans.* Since the public rightly wants universal care, we must focus on how to throw sand into the spending machine.

HOW TO CUT COSTS

In all the debate over national health insurance, one significant fact is obscured: The federal government is already the largest player in American health care. The old, the poor, and the military already have "socialized medicine." Medicaid and Medicare, plus programs for soldiers and veterans, account for 42 percent of all money spent on health. The only real debate is how the rest of us can enjoy a piece of the action.

Another fact about government spending on health is better known: It is a budget-busting monster. Unless something is done to curb rising health costs, which are eating up more and more of the national output every year, there will be no money left in the budget for anything else.

Whatever medical reforms we make, we will have to control the spiraling costs. Here's how:

- If we opt for the managed-care approach, the government can simply reduce costs by cranking down the level of payments made to HMOs. An independent "Federal Health Expenditure Board" could set national health spending goals and negotiate recommended rates of payment with health-care providers. This has been proposed by Maine's Democratic senator George Mitchell.

- Alternatively, we could set firm limits on overall health-care spending. House Ways and Means Committee chairman Dan Rostenkowski, Democrat of Illinois, would limit the annual growth in both public and private health spending to the growth in GNP and authorize the government to set nationwide fees for doctors, hospitals, and other providers at whatever level was necessary to adhere to that restriction.

Studies done by nonpartisan groups that advise Congress on health issues have found that costs could be reduced by as much as $40 billion a year if private insurers paid hospitals and physicians the same rate they are paid by Medicare.

▪ Establishing a single insurer and eliminating our fifteen hundred or so individual insurance companies would save more money than that off the bat. The General Accounting Office has said that eliminating the huge sum now spent on administrative expenses would save enough money to cover the costs of everyone now lacking health insurance.

▪ We could make it harder for people to sue doctors. We hear a lot about the need to reform malpractice law, although no one really knows how much unnecessary and expensive medical care is a result of our present litigious system. There is no doubt that doctors are saddled with excessive malpractice premiums and are forced into "defensive" medicine, although it is also true that ordering extra tests and expensive procedures happens to be quite profitable for doctors.

But before we narrow patients' ability to seek legal recourse against medical incompetence or abuse, we need to put in place a better system of monitoring the quality of medical care. According to studies by the Rand Corporation, as much as one fourth of hospital days, one fourth of medical procedures, and two fifths of medications prescribed may be unnecessary. Many costly medical tests and procedures are administered before their effectiveness has been proven. Dr. Robert H. Brook of Rand, an expert on medical effectiveness, believes that the country could save as much as *40 percent* of health-care costs by eliminating inappropriate or ineffective care.

The government has established an Agency for

Health Care Policy and Research, which has begun gathering data in preparation for developing guidelines for Medicare. Meanwhile, the AMA and Rand have jointly developed "practice parameters" for selected medical procedures, as have numerous specialty societies.

Once guidelines are in place, perhaps the government and private insurers could refuse to pay for procedures that don't meet their recommendations.

• Plain old consumer information could help too. Most people do more research on buying a car than they do before an operation. And neither doctors nor hospitals have any incentive to compete on the basis of lowest-cost quality care, since most consumers don't pay their own bills. But what if one hospital or one surgeon has a much higher death rate than others for comparable operations? People might surely care to know that, and the government (or whoever is paying the bills) could be required to put an institution off-limits if its death rates rose significantly above the norm.

Such monitoring is now possible in Pennsylvania, where the state's Health Care Cost Containment Council publishes mortality rates for every hospital in the state, procedure by procedure. (There are surprising differences.) The statistics are adjusted to account for patients' age and how sick they were when admitted. In 1993, the council, which has been known to hand out T-shirts advising CHECK IT OUT BEFORE YOU CHECK IN, plans to begin releasing individual physicians' track records.

These efforts could be duplicated in every state, using readily available government data. And why not establish a consumers' report on hospitals and doctors, with a toll-free number to call?

• The amount of pure fraud and billing abuse in this country's health system would cover the medical bills of the whole continent of Africa. By some estimates, doctors submit as much as $75 billion a year in inflated claims. According to the General Accounting Office, by 1995 doctors' abuses could cost *$100 billion a year*, taking into account overcharging, billing for services not given, unnecessary tests, and accepting kickbacks for referring patients to cronies' clinics and test laboratories. As the government picks up roughly 40 percent of the nation's medical bills, the taxpayers are being bilked of tens of billions of dollars. Individual consumers pay for much of the rest in higher medical insurance rates.

These estimates do not even include the damage done by fly-by-night medical-insurance companies that no regulator ever heard of. These operators take the public for uncounted billions in medical premiums and then skip out on the claims.

It would be easier to combat criminal health fraud if there were only a single insurer with uniform paperwork, codified treatment definitions, and limits on reimbursements that would eliminate much of the opportunity for overbilling. But even then, we would still need an all-out enforcement effort. Why not use the racketeering laws, which permit seizure and confiscation of property related to misdeeds? Why not staff every federal district attorney's office with a squad of investigators specializing in medical fraud? The government could pay a bounty to anyone who helps uncover an abuse (nurses and technicians could use the extra money), and the investigators could be paid bonuses based on whatever savings they generated for the government.

Republican governor William Weld of Massachusetts has created a new team in his attorney general's office, dedicated to uncovering fraud in claims for workman's compensation. Why can't the country mount a similar crackdown on dishonest doctors and insurance companies? The authorities don't seem to have any trouble finding the resources to go after rioters and street criminals—where is their resolve to act against the much more costly "crime in the suites"? All that would take, to use a rather crude medical term, is guts.

Children:
It's Their
Turn

THE KINDEST CUT

Establishing a means test for entitlements would give us the resources to establish one new entitlement: the right of every American child to a decent standard of living. We are far from that rock-bottom indicator of a self-respecting, forward-looking society.

Right now, one child out of five in this country lives in poverty, and is almost three times as likely to be poor as a senior citizen—the most extreme age disparity anywhere in the world.

The ostensible reason for the age gap is Social Security, an entitlement that has been indexed since 1972 to keep pace with inflation. The program keeps eight out of ten old people who would otherwise be poor out of poverty.

In contrast, the principal program for poor children, Aid to Families with Dependent Children—otherwise known as welfare—is not an entitlement. Far from it. The scapegoat of every rage and envy and frustration bedeviling the population, welfare has been cut in real terms by 42 percent since 1970, and is now able to lift out of poverty not even one of three children it reaches. The problem poor children have, someone once said, is that they come attached to parents no one likes very much.

There is no use arguing about welfare—a program so detested ought to be changed, whatever the facts may be. But that means that we have to come up with another way to rescue millions of children from poverty. Because the degree to which they will live useful, productive lives will determine the quality of all our lives, and our children's future standard of living.

Nobody's going anywhere.

One idea is a pro-family tax cut, called the Refundable Children's Tax Credit. It was proposed in 1991 by the National Commission on Children, a blue-ribbon presidential panel chaired by West Virginia Democratic senator John D. Rockefeller IV. The idea became part of a sweeping legislative package for children introduced in the Senate by Rockefeller and in the House by New York Democrat Thomas J. Downey, another leading congressional advocate for children. Rockefeller's Family Income Security Act of 1992 would refund $1000 to every family for each child; Downey's version of the bill would refund $800 per child. If the pressures for a tax cut prove to be too much for the politicians to resist, this is the one to go for.

First, it is progressive. The flat $1000 credit is worth three times as much to those in the lowest tax brackets than to upper-income taxpayers. In striking contrast, the Bush administration backed a child tax *exemption* that would offer twice as much relief for rich parents as for those in the middle class, and nothing at all for poor parents who pay little or no taxes. (That's not even trickle-down; that's in-your-face, kids.)

Second, the credit for families corrects a major inequity in the tax system. It addresses a bizarre forty-year trend that has increasingly shifted the tax burden *onto* parents of dependent children—could this be yet another reflection of the fact that mothers don't make the tax laws? At every income level, households with dependent children now pay a larger share of the total tax burden than they did in the late 1940s.

Back in 1948, the United States, like every other industrialized nation, had a de facto family allowance that helped offset the cost of raising a child. In those post–World War II days, we seemed to recognize that raising one's children was as valuable a national service as going overseas and killing someone else's.

In accordance with the idea that the government should not tax away that portion of a family's income that is needed to raise children, U.S. tax laws featured an exemption of $600 per child in 1948. At that time, the median family income was $3187, and a family of four at the median income level paid 0.3 percent of its income in federal income taxes. Today, a family at the median level pays 9.1 percent of its income in federal taxes, plus state and local taxes that didn't exist in 1948.

Taxes are supposed to be related to ability to pay. But ask any struggling middle-class parents if their current tax reduction of some $345 a year per child is enough to feed a dog, much less a child.

Finally, the ultimate beauty of the tax credit is that it helps *all* children, including the one in five who lives in poverty. Many children's advocates have concluded that the only way to provide poor kids with a real safety net is with a popular, universal program, like the tax credit, that can do for children what Social Security has done for the elderly.

Anyone who has any income at all and fills out a tax form

would get a sizable sum in the mail from the IRS for every child under age 19 living at home.

In the spring of 1992, Congress actually passed an abbreviated version of the children's tax credit which would have refunded $300 per child for households at or below the median income level. But even this modest step was vetoed by George Bush.

The president was out of step on this one, for it seems that the public is ready at last to do something about the plight of poor children (so long as we don't call it welfare). In early 1992, a poll commissioned by a child-advocacy group found that concern about the health and well-being of children had risen to the top of the voters' budgetary priority list, outdistancing drugs, the environment, and lowering taxes. Almost two thirds of those asked said that they wouldn't mind paying *more* taxes for children's programs. That's good, because the refundable child tax credit alone could amount to $40.3 billion per year.

How can we even consider that kind of outlay, given the state of the nation's finances? What on earth could we be buying that is worth such a cost? Certainly no amount of money can buy good parents. What could a family tax cut buy?

Would it ease the financial burdens of millions of middle- and low-income families?

Better than any competing tax-cut idea, according to advocates.

How many poor children would it lift out of poverty?

This isn't clear. The National Commission on Children will say that a $1000 refundable tax credit, combined with a child-support insurance system (stepped-up enforcement of child support backed by a government-guaranteed minimum benefit of $1500 per year for the first child, $1000 for the second child, and $500 for all subsequent children), would reduce the welfare rolls by about 40 to 42 percent.

Would these kids therefore feel more secure, suffer less stress, do better in school, do less drugs, commit fewer crimes, have more hope?

Probably, according to virtually all the experts on early childhood.

Would this give the rest of us greater security, not to mention savings on locks and police and prisons and remedial education and welfare and all the rest of the dreary drain—money spent too late, after the child is broken?

Maybe.

Is this worth $40 billion a year?

You decide.

■ ■ ■

At a recent international conference, Senator Daniel Patrick Moynihan, Democrat of New York, was bemoaning the enormous number of children reliant on Aid to Families with Dependent Children.

A Frenchman in the audience was puzzled. "I don't understand what is the problem," he whispered. "In France, *all* children have an allowance from the government."

SOCIAL SECURITY FOR KIDS

Of all the groups "entitled" to some protection from the world's harshness, surely helpless children have the most worthy claim. Edward Zigler, a professor of psychology at Yale and one of the founders of Head Start, has suggested that we expand Social Security to include children, thereby insuring the vulnerable beginning of life as well as the dependent final years.

His plan would allow parents, whatever their income, to take a credit against their Social Security of up to five thousand dollars for the first year of their child's life. Either parent could then afford to stay at home or pay for high-quality child care during the critical period when a child most needs close and caring supervision.

The plan would cost the government nothing; it would just shift personal resources toward the younger generation. It would also allow parents to pay back Social Security, so that their income in old age would not suffer.

"People talk about investing in human capital," said Zigler in an interview, "but we are the *only* industrialized country that doesn't have paid infant-care leave. Many Third World countries even have paid leave for parents to care for infants. Yet fifty-four percent of mothers with babies under one year of age work outside the home, and between fifty and seventy percent of them leave their children in settings that are poor in quality. . . . It's a national tragedy. . . . I'm very pragmatic; this is an idea that wouldn't cost anyone but the parents anything."

Of course, the scheme wouldn't help the children of the very poorest parents, who don't pay Social Security. A complementary idea, then, is to allow poor pregnant women to enter federally funded child-development centers that would offer either residential or day programs. Democratic senator Bill Bradley of New Jersey, a supporter of this idea, says that a pilot program would cost between one and two billion dollars a year.

EARLY START, EVEN START

Everyone knows that the best way to tackle the country's major social and economic problems—drugs, welfare, crime, and the despair that breeds them—is to start with the youngest children. The rioters in Los Angeles, said Texas governor Ann Richards, "were once our children."

It is impossible to prove, in hard-boiled economic terms, that a literal investment in children's well-being can prevent social ills and produce hardworking, creative, law-abiding taxpayers twenty years down the road. But child-development authorities agree that the crucial formative experiences take place by the age of four. If they are right, and the evidence is compelling that one's self-image and personality are well established by that tender age, then we need to reconsider how soon public education must begin.

The well-off among us must clearly believe that earlier is better as far as education is concerned, because the great majority of affluent and middle-class kids are already toddling off with their lunch boxes by the time they are three. In contrast, only 40 percent of low-income three- and four-year-olds attend preschool—yet another aspect of the growing gap between the haves and the have-nots in the United States.

What disadvantaged children really need, many child advocates believe, is development centers for themselves *and* their mothers—an idea that is better than its label: "two-generational programming."

"In the old days, we used to say, 'Give us children for a few hours a day and we'll save them,' " says Wade Horn, the senior federal administrator for Head Start. "Now we know that . . . if we are going to save children, we have to save the family, and that means working with the parents."

Many of the educational and social gains registered by children in Head Start fade or disappear within two years, not because the program has failed, but because it is just not enough. All evidence indicates that seriously disadvantaged children need earlier intervention, for longer periods of time, *with* parental involvement.

The models for successful prevention programs do exist. There is no mystery about "what works."

One promising initiative is Even Start, the major federal effort in the growing family-literacy movement. Even Start targets children from birth to age seven and brings them into programs with a parent, usually the mother, who is taught basic academic subjects and child-rearing skills while her youngsters are in preschool or the early grades.

Is this adult education important? The latest estimate of the number of adults who are functionally illiterate—meaning that they cannot do everyday tasks such as balance a checkbook—is twenty-five million. Some forty-five million adults can barely read a newspaper or follow written instructions on the job. When these people have children, they often pass those inadequacies on, and it is hard if not impossible for any school system to counter so strong a negative influence.

If we could turn those parents on to learning, and to the future that greater competence and independence can promise, we have a chance to save not one, but two generations.

At Even Start, parents and children go to school together four mornings a week. They eat breakfast together, share music, story, and writing time, and then the kids head for their play groups while the parents go off for language, math, or science instruction. Many work on their General Educational Development, or high school equivalency, certificates.

In a 1991 study of fourteen Even Start–type programs in Indiana, West Virginia, and Kentucky, the National Center for Family Literacy found that children who participated as preschoolers were less likely to need special-education services later on, and were overwhelmingly rated by their elementary school teachers as eager to learn. (In contrast, a recent survey of seven thousand kindergarten teachers concluded that 35 percent of all American kids enter school unprepared.)

None of the children from the monitored family programs had been held back a grade, even though 25 percent of children from similar backgrounds typically fail at least one grade before fourth grade.

One of the added benefits of such programs is that the close contact with parents inspires administrators to help families with some of their other problems. One Even Start coordinator in Prince Georges County, Maryland, near Washington, D.C., said that he and his associates "did a little bit of everything," interceding in evictions, providing emergency food and clothing, sitting in with parents at school conferences, and helping with jobs, immigration, and health crises.

Now that we know these programs are effective, it is time to move beyond the "demonstration" stage. In 1991, there were only 233 Even Start projects around the country, serving fewer than twenty thousand people. There are roughly three thousand family-literacy programs nationwide. That is ten times the number that existed five years ago, but still ridiculously inadequate compared to what is needed.

Another way to reach the "two generations" is simply to expand the family-support and literacy programs of Head Start. More than one third of today's Head Start staff members are parents of current or former students—and family involvement helps explain how the program has survived all of these years. Forty-one Head Start centers today offer parents counseling and referral services in literacy, job training, and substance abuse. Roughly one hundred Head Start programs provide parental instruction on infant care and child devel-

[92]   KILLING THE SACRED COWS

opment. Virtually everyone in the early-childhood field believes that these services should be an integral part of all fifteen hundred Head Start programs.

The problem, as always, is money.

Head Start, as popular as it is, only serves 28 percent of all eligible children. To reach all eligible three- to five-year-olds, Head Start will need $8 billion, $5.2 billion more than it is now getting. Enlarging the mission to include two generations might raise the price tag to $10 billion a year.

Where on earth will the money come from?

How about from state prison budgets?

Many states now spend more on prisons than they spend on education. The cost of keeping a person in prison for a year hovers around $20,000; the cost of one year of public education is roughly $5,000. Spending more money to lock people up than we spend on educating them is akin to spending more money on people's medical needs in their last year of life than in their infancy (which is, as it happens, how we do it in this country).

Why don't state legislatures require that a set portion of every dollar allocated to the prison system has to be spent on programs for children under six? One tenth, say, of the $20 billion spent on incarceration every year ought to go for prevention, to early-childhood programs that we know can prevent later social pathology.

Every time the prisons get a dollar, the kids should get a dime: Call it "two-generational law enforcement." If the idea forces states to seek out cheaper means of punishment, fine, because incarceration is the most costly, least effective way to handle the majority of criminals who are nonviolent.

The money now being spent on remedial education could also be a source of funds. Currently, the major program helping poor children in the early grades costs about $7 billion a year, mostly for tutoring. Many argue that remedial-education money would be better spent on prevention, before children at risk of learning problems get to school.

Expanded early-childhood programs could be staffed not only by parents but also by members of a national service corps and a senior service corps. Such "cheap labor" could help make a comprehensive, universal early-education system feasible.

Still another idea on how to pay for early education was proposed in 1990 by then Oregon governor Neil Goldschmidt, who requested an amendment to the state constitution that would dedicate 30 percent of Oregon's lottery revenues to guarantee that Head Start would be available to every child in the state. He called it a "drug prevention" measure.

Maybe some of our new female officeholders will pick up on these ideas and make them happen. Many women understand this kind of "home economics" better than men do, and know that well-nurtured children are fundamentally more important to a thriving nation than are pieces of equipment or buildings or even capital.

Neglecting children amounts to a statement of hopelessness. When a family neglects its children, it self-destructs. When a whole country neglects its children—economically, educationally, or emotionally—its future is in jeopardy as well.

· VI ·

Education: The Best Choices

CHARTER SCHOOLS

Of all the hidebound institutions in America, few are more intransigent and less responsive to those they are supposed to serve than the big-city public school bureaucracies. In many places the public school system has become a stepping-stone to power for politicians. Administrative offices and custodial systems have become troughs of pork patronage; as a result, many if not most major urban school systems now have more support personnel than teachers.

Lowest on the totem pole are the children.

Frustration with the urban schools, and flight from them, has been building for two decades; and slowly but steadily, the public sentiment about what should be done about them has become more radical.

After the 1983 release of the influential Carnegie Foundation report *Nation at Risk*, the cry was for more spending, better teachers, and higher standards. All of these were and still are needed, but it is apparent that they are not enough. Even Albert Shanker of the American Federation of Teachers has accused the public school system of "taking its customers for granted." There have been bold calls for school restructuring—by granting teachers professional status, giving individual schools autonomy through self-management, and introducing limited open enrollment. Nagging suspicions remain, however, that these suggested reforms don't really strike at the heart of the problem.

By the end of the 1980s, the buzzword had become "choice." Choice, of course, has existed for years; any kid can go to any school, provided his or her parents can afford private school tuition or the cost of moving. The choice movement today is about extending the option to all children, including the poor kids who are the captive clients of the troubled big-city public schools. The hope is that introducing competition can do what bureaucratic school management has not been able to do: put children first.

The idea has spread like a cold in a kindergarten. The choice movement is growing in Europe, and in the United States public opinion has dramatically shifted in its favor. And who could be surprised? Americans expect choice—concerning the products they buy, the neighborhoods in which they live, the jobs they take. Why shouldn't they demand at least some choice in determining the kind of school their children attend? In a consumer society, and in an era when people from Eastern Europe to China are demanding more flexible institutions, the question is inevitable.

A 1990 Gallup poll for *Kappan* magazine showed that public school choice was favored by 62 percent of Americans, up from only 12 percent ten years earlier. Sixty-five percent of parents with children in public schools supported choice. Not surprisingly, since upper-income whites had already exercised choice by largely abandoning the public schools, blacks expressed *their* eagerness to share the privilege: 72 percent favored choice.

Perhaps most telling—and a sign of things to come—support for choice was highest among the young: 72 percent of those aged eighteen to twenty-nine approved (compared to 54 percent over the age of fifty).

Almost half those polled supported the voucher system (the use of public funds to finance attendance at private and parochial schools), a sign that the public school system—and the sense of community it fosters—is deeply threatened.

An example of what can happen when the powers that be fail to respond to public sentiment occurred in Milwaukee, where about twenty public schools on the city's North Side are all black. The black community asked the school district and the state for a separate district they could run themselves. They were turned down. With that, State Representative Polly Williams, a black former welfare mother, put through the legislature a bill opening the way for inner-city children to attend private schools at public expense. Under the program, about one thousand poor children are eligible to receive vouchers to attend private, nonsectarian schools in Milwaukee.

But the voucher idea does not have to be the focal point of the choice debate. The idea is anathema to most educators and everyone concerned with preserving one of the few remaining American institutions in which a unifying common culture can still be fostered. Vouchers would place an intolerable new burden on stretched public school budgets by subsidizing families who would, or already do, send their children to private schools. And it is debatable whether a voucher program that included parochial schools, by far the largest category of private schools, would be compatible with the constitutional separation of church and state.

The issue ought to be how to create meaningful choices

within the public school system itself. As of this writing, more than twenty states are trying some version of public school choice.

Some of these efforts have shown real results. After years of allowing students a choice among public schools, a low-income minority school district in the East Harlem section of Manhattan went from being the worst in New York City in terms of reading achievement to one that is now performing near the citywide average. In 1974, 15 percent of the district's children read at grade level, less than half the citywide average. In 1988, 62.5 percent of its students were reading at or above grade level, only 2.5 percent below average.

It is increasingly clear, however, that choice alone is not a panacea, that enduring reform won't come unless the ultimate sacred cow—the school districts' monopoly on public education—is sacrificed.

The real revolution entails getting school districts out of the business of owning *and* operating *all* public schools. The current system, with its superintendent, its bureaucracy, its stultifying rules and procedures, its guaranteed revenues, and its captive clientele, trapped in the system whether or not they learn anything, is the core of the problem. In schools, as in so many other institutions, the age of the centralized, entrenched organization run by apparatchiks determined to preserve their sinecures should be history.

Up to now, the school debate has been framed by two extreme alternatives: Either we send all education money to the public school superintendents, or we send vouchers to parents. But there are other possible approaches.

One is sometimes called "diversification." If a district insists on continuing to own and operate schools, a community can break the monopoly by saying, Fine, but you won't any longer be the *only* owner/operator of our public schools. In 1991, this approach was sanctioned in Minnesota with the passage of

the charter schools law, which allows parents and educators
to contract *any* school board to set up an autonomous public
school, which children can attend without charge.

In theory, the chartering body could include a variety of
public agencies, including public colleges and universities, local and state governments, social-service agencies, and even
public zoos and museums.

Under Minnesota's law, the new schools will operate
through contracts with the chartering school board, which
will set objectives and monitor performance of the otherwise independent schools. The state will set only minimal requirements beyond adherence to civil rights, student rights,
nonsectarian instruction, health and safety standards, and student performance criteria. Private schools will be kept out of
the scheme.

The new schools will be accountable to their chartering
bodies and, through choice, to families. All applicants will be
given an equal chance to enroll in any public school, subject
to limits of space—although a new school could specialize in
a particular field or in children with some special characteristic.

One of the first proposals generated by the new law is to
create a day school in the Twin Cities for deaf children. Up
to now, the only choice deaf children had was to attend a
special state-run boarding school or to be mainstreamed into
conventional classrooms.

The charter idea is spreading. By the summer of 1992,
proposals for similar reforms had been introduced in the legislatures of Michigan, Tennessee, Colorado, and Massachusetts.

A second alternative to the school-district monopoly would
allow a district to continue to own its public schools but not
to operate them. Outside entrepreneurs would contract with
the district to run some of its schools.

One private company, Education Alternatives, Inc. (EAI), of Bloomington, Minnesota, already runs private schools in Minnesota and Arizona, and a public school in Miami. In the fall of 1992, EAI took over the day-to-day operations of nine Baltimore public schools. The new arrangement, which affects 5100 of Baltimore's 110,000 students, features "open" classrooms in which students work in small, informal groups, with individually tailored study requirements, pupil participation in daily classroom planning, and enhanced parental involvement. Instead of "a sage on the stage," as one company executive put it, the classroom will have "a guide on the side."

The participating schools, eight elementary and one middle school, were selected in part because school administrators and community activists had indicated interest. The arrangement will be implemented for five years, although the school system has the right to cancel the program at any time. EAI is obligated to operate the nine schools at a cost not to exceed what Baltimore would otherwise have spent on them. The company hopes to make its profit by cutting costs not directly related to education; by making school buildings more energy efficient, for instance.

A third, even more radical, approach would convert the school district into a kind of "policy board" that neither owns nor operates its schools, but acts as a buyer of educational services from independent organizations.

Well-publicized ventures like Whittle Communications' Edison Project could eventually become educational contractors to public school systems, although the stated intention of the project is to build a nationwide system of one thousand *private* schools that operate at about the same per-pupil cost as public schools.

No one can say at the moment what new form public education will take, and different systems may well find their own unique solutions. But fundamental change in public education is already reflected in the many ideas that are being tested on a small scale all over the country. By all measures —the sentiment of parents, the low test scores and lack of preparedness of too many children, the costs of educational bureaucracies—radical changes are necessary. And in the long run, changes that are necessary do tend to happen, especially in democracies.

THE BOX AS TEACHER

Did you realize that the commercial television networks do not devote even a single hour a week to preschool programming?

What does that have to do with the economy, you might inquire?

Everything. Preschool children spend more time in front of TV sets than they spend with their parents or teachers. With older children, television has replaced reading, music lessons, sports, and homework as *the* after-school activity. And it is hurting their academic performance vis-à-vis their peers in other countries.

A major study (*The International Assessment of Educational Progress*, funded by the U.S. Education Department, the National Science Foundation, and the Carnegie Foundation) comparing the math and science skills of American nine- and thirteen-year-olds with those of students from fourteen other countries found that while the younger American children tested relatively well in science, they lagged in math. By age thirteen, U.S. kids ranked near the bottom in both subjects. The study also found that small class size, a longer school year, and more money spent on books, computers, and teacher salaries did *not* correlate with student achievement. What did show a correlation was *time spent watching television*. "Within all these countries, the more time students spend watching television, the less well they do in science," said one of the study's authors.

Ernest Boyer of the Carnegie Foundation for the Advancement of Teaching declared: "It is my deep conviction that education and the economy are inextricably interlocked, and if we do not begin to invest more fully in our human resources—most especially in our youngest children—both the economic and civic vitality of the nation will decline."

What can we do? Oregon's Democratic congressman Ron Wyden has introduced legislation that would require the networks to air one hour a week of educational programming. Every family-oriented network show would also have to carry one minute of public service announcements (promoting reading or school attendance, for example). Wyden's bill would also take steps toward encouraging more preschool programming on public television and the creation of cable channels for children.

We ought to be going much further than this. One hour a week is far too little. One hour a *day* isn't enough—and that's the *least* the networks ought to be required to air for children. Why aren't the conservatives who attack public television and are the loudest in their support for family values demanding that funding for public TV be tied to the amount of educational programming it provides? And funding should be devoted in part to developing a series of entertaining and informative shows that could be run on any number of cable channels.

Parents have power here. Don't wait for Congress; start putting pressure on your local network affiliate station to comply with these guidelines *now*.

The public can also move for a reduction of violence on *all* television shows, especially, of course, children's programs.

(According to the National Coalition on Television Violence, Saturday-morning programming contains, on average, twenty-six acts of violence every sixty minutes.)

All that it would take is for some group to rate TV shows, just as is done with movies, and to call for a boycott of the sponsors of all shows that hit an X rating on the violence chart. If you want to see the business of delivering TV audiences to advertisers develop a social conscience, watch how quickly producers would respond to just a hint of a national boycott.

If this is going too far for your taste, here's another idea: Why not disallow a certain amount of ad time for every incidence of violence on a television show? Say, five seconds' worth of commercials have to go if the script contains a slugging; ten seconds less of ad time sold for every rape or killing depicted. Although such a system might be hard to enforce, we have to think of *something* to improve the performance of a private, for-profit, regulated industry that happens to be, after ourselves, our children's most important teacher.

THE GREAT TRAINING ROBBERY

The United States badly needs nationally accredited technical and professional training, already a routine part of the educational system throughout Western Europe, for every high school graduate not going on to college.

The kids who don't attend college have been called "the forgotten half," but in fact they are the majority of American young people. Only 40 percent of college-age Americans get any higher education.

What are these kids prepared to do? For the most part, their educational experience has had no relationship to the job market. Less than one eighth of high school graduates have any vocational preparation for the job they enter. And most American employers have no interest in training them, given the risk that they will just take their skills and find a better-paying job somewhere else.

In this regard, young people are treated no differently than most adult workers. Aside from a few companies like Xerox, IBM, and Motorola, most American firms barely train *any* of their front-line employees, preferring to view labor primarily as a cost to be minimized. American auto workers, for example, receive less than fifty hours of training on employment, while a newly hired Japanese auto worker gets over three hundred hours of training in his first six months.

In a slow economy, when companies are laying off skilled workers, it is even harder to find an employer who is willing to hire and train an unskilled youth.

The effects of this neglect became painfully apparent during the 1980s, as the wages of the bottom 40 percent of male workers actually fell. And because they can contribute so little to the wealth-building process, these poorly trained people bring down overall productivity and the standard of living. Indeed, they *cost* money. How many teenagers figure that dead-end, low-paying jobs aren't enough, and decide to deal drugs? How many become alienated, and work at half their capacity or wind up in jail? It would be infinitely smarter and more humane for society to devise apprenticeship programs for young, future blue-collar workers while they are still in high school.

Moreover, in the new international economic ball game, the most competitive companies will be those with creative flexibility, a quality that requires highly trained people who can think for themselves, work in problem-solving teams, and be fast on their feet. That kind of organizational dynamism doesn't flourish in a climate that treats the average high school graduate like a breathing robot.

American kids can surely be turned into one of the most skilled cadres of workers in the world. If the army can do it, our private companies can do it. Our young people performed admirably in the Gulf War after joining the military for the training and opportunities they couldn't find in the private economy. But we don't need their skills in a huge standing army anymore; we need them to compete in the post–Cold War global economy.

Many of the nation's governors would like to see an American version of the successful German youth-apprenticeship programs, which are credited with turning out a sophisticated and productive work force. In 1990, the average hourly wage in Germany was $21.30 an hour, versus $14.83 in the United States, but German goods were still highly competitive internationally. And German students who had finished secondary school in the lower half of their class were far better paid, in a wider variety of jobs, than their American counterparts.

A German-style apprenticeship program, enrolling high school juniors in three- or four-year work-study programs, could be implemented in this country at a minimal cost to the government. Here's what an American version might look like:

- At the end of the tenth grade, students would choose between work-oriented apprenticeships and the purely academic track. *All* sixteen-year-old students would have to have met a world-class performance standard of basic skills, including reading, math, English, science, history, and economics. The federal government has already called for such a national standard, and a number of states are moving to implement it.

- In the eleventh grade, those who have chosen apprenticeships would begin a three-year program. They would combine school courses and on-the-job training with a formally contracted employer.

- At the end of twelfth grade, apprentices would be tested for job and educational proficiency.
- The following year, apprentices would spend at least 75 percent of their time on the job, and the remainder in technical training.
- A new Youth Apprenticeship Institute, staffed by representatives of business, labor, government, and schools, would set standards for entry into the full range of service and manufacturing occupations. High schools, community colleges, and training institutions would offer courses for accreditation, while the Institute would monitor work sites to ensure that apprentices were receiving appropriate on-the-job training.

As in Germany, most of the direct cost of this program should be borne by employers, although companies would be permitted to pay a less-than-market wage for trainees. State and local governments would fund the development, testing, and monitoring of the system, partly out of savings from existing vocational-education programs. The cost to taxpayers, especially when measured against the gain, qualifies this idea as one of the greatest bargains imaginable.

PLAY OR PAY OR ELSE

Apprenticeships will never take off in America, however, unless employers are *required* to participate or contribute financially—to play or pay. Most big American companies are quite comfortable with apprenticeships, for they operate them in their German factories. They don't do it here because they don't have to.

In the United States, support for the youth-training concept has been building for a few years: Pilot projects have been funded; several states have commissioned studies; Oregon has already passed legislation adopting a comprehensive school-to-work program. But thus far, not much has happened in the private sector, except among some hospitals, chronically short of technicians, and some manufacturers, in desperate need of skilled machinists and metalworkers.

In Germany, employers are required to pay 3.5 percent of payroll to public training and employment schemes, and virtually every industrialized country has a substantial payroll tax-supported fund to finance workers' continuing education. Only the United States lacks such a fund.

American employers do spend almost 1.5 percent of payroll on training, but an estimated 70 percent of that money is spent on the top 10 percent of the work force, often on minimally disguised managerial perks. (I once ran into a business conference in Vail, Colorado, where the attending executives gathered for a breakfast meeting every day before pouring out onto the slopes, where they remained until late afternoon. "All tax deductible," one assured me.)

Legislation introduced in Congress has called on firms with twenty or more employees to contribute 1 to 2 percent of payroll to in-house apprenticeship and training programs. Any company not spending the full mandated amount would have to contribute the difference to a new Skills Development Fund that would train part-time, dislocated, and disadvantaged workers. (One percent of American payroll in 1989 was approximately $30 billion.)

This proposal left it entirely up to employers how they would spend their training funds. But representatives of big business, including the National Association of Manufacturers, quickly weighed in against any suggestion of making play-or-pay compulsory. Even a bill bribing employers with a tax credit to set up apprenticeship programs died in the last Congress.

At bottom, the fundamental obstacle to youth training is the same policy that hampers American productivity growth:

Most U.S. companies are not in the habit of constantly upgrading their operations, modernizing and fine-tuning their production processes in a way that would require a steady pool of skilled workers. If companies do need new skills, they often just shift the work overseas. As a financial services executive told the Commission on the Skills of the American Work Force: "I can do my back-office functions anywhere in the world now. If I can't get enough skilled workers here, I'll move the skilled jobs out of the country and just do the customer interface here."

What a national commitment! What a way to build a great country!

In the name of patriotism and American productivity, and for the sake of the "forgotten half," here are a few carrots and sticks to get a national apprenticeship program rolling:

- Make it mandatory. *Require* that companies with twenty or more employees invest at least 1.5 percent of payroll in training young apprentices and front-line workers. Any training of executives would be financed above and beyond that level.
- *Require* that all employers pay a small surtax on their unemployment insurance tax, the money to be earmarked for the national apprenticeship program. (A similar policy has existed in California since the early 1980s.)
- Mandate works councils within each factory or office to implement the apprenticeship program.
- And for a sweetener, let's introduce a Block Investment Credit. Today we give companies a tax break for investing in plants and equipment but nothing for investing in worker skills. This is increasingly anachronistic: As a recent study put it, "Investments in physical assets represent a declining portion of overall corporate

investment. The other, 'softer' forms of investment are of growing importance to competition. . . ."

"Soft" investments include R&D, employee training, information systems, and organizational development. A block tax credit could cover all these intangible as well as tangible forms of investment.

The credit would apply only to that amount of investment exceeding some three-year average period, so it wouldn't be given for investments that would have been made anyway. Since small businesses create most of the jobs but do the least training, their base would be the lowest and their incentive the greatest. And since skills training involves what economists call "externalities," that is, spillovers that create benefits for society as a whole (as distinct from private returns to a firm's owners), there is a good case for having society help pay for it.

· VII ·

Volunteering

NATIONAL SERVICE

When I told people that I was writing about fresh economic ideas, many asked whether I was including national volunteer service. After all the fractured politics, social divisiveness, and dog-eat-dog materialism of the 1980s, there seems to be a real hunger for shared national purpose and a restored sense of community. People seem to understand that we aren't going to make it as a nation unless we can recreate a civic life that binds us together. National service wouldn't be a cure-all, but it would be a wonderful place to start.

In his 1988 book *A Call to Civic Service*, Charles C. Moskos, a professor of sociology at Northwestern University, neatly described what a civilian service could do: work that is neglected because there is no profit in it for the private sector and because the government can't afford it.

Much of this is the kind of volunteer "labor of love" that women have always performed, unpaid and unsung, that we have lost as women have rightfully moved into full paying professions. How appropriate if we could now acknowledge that such *pro bono* work is so critical to our society that *all* of us should contribute time to it during our lives.

Imagine millions of volunteers as tutors, mentors, and teachers' aides in preschool and literacy programs; aides in hospitals, hospices, and community clinics; teachers in child-care centers; providers of in-home care and driver's services for the elderly and infirm; staff for shelters for the homeless and for battered women; workers rehabilitating low-income housing; operators of drug and suicide hot lines; recyclers; caretakers of public spaces, clearing urban gardens, planting trees, building recreational facilities and bike paths; reforesters; police reservists and civilian patrolers; tutors in correctional facilities; makers of Braille and talking books; and aides in microfilming hundreds of thousands of volumes in the Library of Congress and major research collections that are crumbling into dust. And that is just a start.

A 1986 Ford Foundation report on national service concluded that nearly 3.5 million positions could be filled by short-term volunteers with no specialized training. Imagine the change in our quality of life if a citizens' corps were mobilized to direct the energy and enthusiasm of youth to help solve some of our most pressing domestic problems.

Administrative costs could be kept to a minimum by attaching most volunteers to public agencies and approved non-profit associations. They could live at home and receive a stipend covering little more than basic expenses and health and life insurance. Charles Moskos estimates that nonresidential programs would cost about $9000 per person (the average cost of a VISTA volunteer) and that residential programs like conservation corps would run about $16,000 per person.

The cost of a program with 600,000 volunteers would of course be determined by the exact mix of jobs chosen, but

Moskos's rough estimate comes to $7 billion, with the states paying about $1.3 billion and the nonprofits contributing $1000 for each volunteer they enroll. To be complete, any budgeting exercise should balance those costs against the value of the work performed, but what is the final value, Moskos asks, "of preserving our physical resources, cleaning up the environment, caring for the elderly and handicapped, rescuing our research collections, staffing our public institutions with citizen servers, and opening new avenues for dead-end youth?"

Weighed against those gains, $7 billion, or even twice that, seems a bargain. Where would the money come from? Out of what we are currently spending on "national defense." With the Cold War over, it is time for service to the country to include civilians as well as the military. It is time to revive William James's notion of a "moral equivalent of war," a purpose capable of calling forth the determination and selflessness evoked by war, without the bloodshed and killing.

In 1988, the Democratic Leadership Council suggested that student aid for higher education be linked to voluntary service. As later enlarged upon by Bill Clinton during the 1992 presidential campaign, any young person who qualified academically could receive a four-year college loan, to be paid back with two years' service in a "domestic Peace Corps" of teachers, police officers, and social workers (or repaid as a small percentage of income withheld like a payroll tax).

This idea of linking education aid and national service has been proposed in the Senate by Sam Nunn and in the House by Oklahoma Democrat Dave McCurdy. They would establish a new citizens' corps that would offer young people a chance to serve one or two years in either a civilian or military capacity at subsistence pay. Each year, they would receive vouchers worth $10,000 for the civilians and $12,000 (reflecting the potentially greater risk) for the military, to be used for education, vocational training, or as a down payment on a first home.

Nunn and McCurdy's proposal would eventually make national service a prerequisite for most students who receive federal student aid, turning college aid from a limited, needs-based entitlement into a much larger, earned benefit available to anyone willing to serve. The Nunn/McCurdy approach makes aid to education dependent upon service. Clinton may have the better idea: make higher education available to all, and let people decide for themselves how to repay the country.

National community service as an idea can stand on its own. It worked in the 1930s—with the Civilian Conservation Corps—and small programs are succeeding all around the country today. In some twenty states, approximately twenty thousand young men and women between the ages of sixteen and twenty-three are employed in mostly nonresidential C.C.C.-type programs, the oldest and largest of which is in California.

With an upsurge of interest in volunteerism, and a scarcity of jobs for young people, twelve new local urban corps have been launched in the past two years. Such programs ought to be expanded nationwide. With a national service corps, revived G.I. bill, and a mandated apprenticeship program, we could give every kid in America a chance to become skilled and useful to society. That is something people wouldn't mind paying taxes for.

As part of this general trend, mandatory student service has spread to about 200 schools nationwide, including the Detroit and Atlanta school systems. Beginning in the fall of 1993, the state of Maryland will require that every high school graduate complete seventy-five hours of community service.

SILVER SERVICE

Today, only 12 percent of men and women over the age of 65 are in the work force, compared with 42 percent in 1950. Many are encouraged to take early retirement years before they are ready, and are penalized by Social Security if they earn a decent salary. Yet the great majority of older people are in good health and would welcome the opportunity to perform rewarding and useful service.

A recent task force in New York City found that more than half of retirees between the ages of 55 and 64 said that they hoped to do something meaningful and productive after 65. Many were willing to consider unpaid work. "Why is it," asked a gerontologist, "that those qualities which are especially associated with middle and later life—experience, accumulated skills, knowledge, wisdom, and perspective—are discarded just when they are coming to fruition in human beings?" We don't mind presidents in their sixties and seventies; why should we mind other workers that age?

In New York, the Retired Senior Volunteer Program dispatches ten thousand volunteers daily to homeless shelters, hospitals, libraries, and museums. Hundreds of older volunteers at one hospital in Harlem care for AIDS babies. At the Better Business Bureau, retirement-age volunteers do everything from answering phones to mediating disputes.

Such a program could be replicated all over the country by communities that are desperate to salvage their social-service programs from budget cuts. Congress is helping by moving to raise the maximum amount that Social Security recipients can earn and still collect full benefits (a measure that will be especially needed if we begin to tax Social Security benefits of the affluent).

What about a Neighborhood Silver Service Corps in every community? What if everyone receiving a Social Security check each month also received a list of service opportunities? What about requiring that every able-bodied retired person up to the age of 75 who receives a check from the government put in an afternoon a week for a specified number of weeks a year with an approved nonprofit organization, school, hospital, or public agency of his choice? The government could pay the minimum wage for the work if it is compulsory.

You can imagine the screams. But my guess is that such a program would, like jury duty, become something everyone complains about but rather enjoys—or at least learns an invaluable lesson from about the world we live in and whom we share it with. Strengthening those connections can only make us stronger.

Dozens of studies have shown that volunteer service programs tend to help those who serve at least as much as those they are supposed to be helping. Volunteers of all ages and social classes seem to gain in self-confidence and develop a stronger sense of community. I discovered this a few years ago while writing a book about the Sanctuary movement, a grass roots, church-based effort to help refugees from Central America. Virtually everyone in the movement whom I interviewed said the same thing: "The refugees did more for me than I ever did for them." This struck me at first as saccharine, but I gradually realized that it was true. The power of altruism has been utterly underestimated in recent years and is, I believe, a force just waiting to be tapped.

We don't need to throw money at social problems; we need to throw people at them.

· VIII ·

The Banks: How to Create a Democratic Money System

DARE TO DREAM

If a nation's budget is the skeleton of a society, its financial institutions are its circulatory system, determining where and to whom its lifeblood—capital—flows. Unfortunately, the United States banking system has an advanced case of hardening of the arteries.

Or perhaps it's cirrhosis of the liver, considering that many of the banks' problems are the result of overindulgence—an orgy of speculation and foolish, greedy lending.

Whatever the ailment, the banks aren't functioning properly. The S&L industry is moribund, too long adrift from its purpose, which was to channel people's savings into affordable housing. The commercial banks are refusing to lend to many credit-worthy businesses, preferring to buy Treasury bills like skittish octogenarians; rebuilding their capital, depleted by loans to the Third World and fly-by-night developers, with fat interest-rate spreads between what they pay depositors and what they can earn on risk-free investments.

Add to that the financial system's persistent failure to allow any drops of precious capital to trickle into the wrong sort of neighborhood, the systemic, well-documented discrimination against minority borrowers, and the banks' growing irrelevance to many participants in the economy, from major corporations, which can raise much of the money they need by issuing their own paper, to consumers, whose spare cash has shifted into mutual funds and other savings vehicles. As a banker friend remarked to me recently, "Who needs banks? Maybe they're obsolete."

He joked, but financial deregulation, credit cronyism, lemminglike lending, and outright fraud have taken their toll. The system we are left with is as rotten as an old cantaloupe. The amazing thing is how few people have concluded that we need to throw it out and get a new one.

Even when the public is stuck with the bill for the biggest bank robbery in American history—mandating a government bailout that could cost every man, woman, and child in America almost two thousand dollars *each*—the debate over bank reform, or "bank deform," as Texas populist Jim Hightower puts it, remains as strait as a one-lane highway on the Fourth of July.

With the subject lost somewhere in a black hole, few Americans can even imagine that we have at the moment a historic opportunity to build a financial system that could actually deliver the goods: credit where it is needed, at reasonable rates, from more stable institutions.

One organization that has been raising the right questions is the Financial Democracy Campaign, a coalition of consumer, labor, and church groups representing millions of citizens (among its member organizations: Citizen Action, the Consumer Federation of America, the United Auto Workers, the Communications Workers of America, the National Council of Churches, the National Education Association, and

Friends of the Earth. The Financial Democracy Campaign has an ambitious goal: to rally a *majority* of Americans around a vision of a democratic financial system and to put fundamental financial reform on the national agenda.

The FDC has turned out studies, speeches, and congressional testimony, and while that populist majority has not quite been assembled yet, the political revolt of 1992 indicates that the possibility of real change in the banking system cannot be ruled out.

The FDC initiated its mission by doing everything it could think of to draw attention to the scandal of the S&L bailout. Supporters have mailed hundreds of brown paper bags to congressmen with the message, "Don't leave me holding the bag." One of the FDC's affiliated groups, Seattle's Bucket Brigade (as in "Don't use my bucket to bail those guys out") shipped squares of carpet to Capitol Hill with the warning, "You can't sweep this under the rug." And on Valentine's Day 1991, FDC demonstrators in twelve cities handed out heart-shaped red lollipops stamped with the message: "I'm sick of being played for a sucker."

"It is too bad we have to reduce ourselves to a fifth-grade level to attract the attention of our elected representatives," one activist told a reporter. "But you need a gimmick to be heard. They worry about people clever enough to have gimmicks."

The FDC is more than clever enough, but they are David up against Goliath, and without a slingshot. As the S&L scandal unfolded, bank PACs pumped $4.5 million into the campaign accounts of members of the congressional banking committees. In the three federal elections up to 1990 political spending by the nation's largest banks grew fifteen times faster than overall PAC spending, according to Federal Election Commission data. It was money well spent.

Originally, the FDC wanted to make sure that the costs of

the big S&L blowout were billed to those who went to the party: the financial industry and the wealthy. To avoid hundreds of billions of dollars in borrowing costs down the road, they wanted the bailout funded on a pay-as-you-go basis. The "pay" part of this was to come from a surtax on the wealthiest taxpayers and a onetime fee on brokerage, securities, and accounting firms.

No dice, said Congress.

The campaign wanted the FDIC to stop covering big uninsured depositors in its bailouts, and to levy an asset-appreciation tax on the profits from any quick resale of foreclosed S&L properties that the government had sold at bargain-basement prices to billionaire investors in 1988.

No dice, said Congress.

Today, the FDC's wish list is still full of what you might call radical common sense. But to most congressmen, these ideas are as welcome as a wet dog in bed. And meanwhile, the campaign's natural allies, the ordinary voters who hate taxes, learn almost nothing from newspapers, television, or radio (including *public* television and radio) about the FDC's ideas and the possibility of getting something in return for that two-thousand-dollar tax on each and every one of us.

Three years into its effort, the campaign has lost almost all its major battles, although it has won some important defensive actions:

- In late 1991, the Administration's effort to eliminate the sixty-year-old barrier between commercial and investment banking was defeated.
- The same legislation allowed the Resolution Trust Corporation to negotiate directly (and exclusively) with nonprofits and public agencies on housing purchases prior to market offerings. The nonprofits are also being offered 5-percent-down RTC financing. This "affordable

housing disposition program" is belatedly becoming "the single greatest opportunity to get affordable housing into the hands of low-income people," according to Congressman Joseph P. Kennedy II of Massachusetts, a legislative sponsor of the program.

• The banking bill introduced some re-regulatory measures, including tougher scrutiny of foreign banks and the assessment of insurance premiums against the foreign deposits of big banks, annual on-site examinations and independent audits, early intervention, a curtailment of the "too big to fail" doctrine that allowed the complete bailout of all depositors in large banks, and the possibility of restricting compensation at undercapitalized institutions.

• A few consumer protection measures were also passed, including a truth-in-savings act mandating more disclosure about the terms and conditions of deposit accounts.

But as FDC chief Tom Schlesinger put it, "We have a long, long way to go—to put it charitably—before we get the hogs out of the creek."

So far, the principal vision of the future of American banking has been the one put forward by the Bush administration, allowing banks to expand across state lines, consolidate into huge megabanks (which analyst Martin Mayer has described as "dinosaurs"), and operate with less regulation than ever, including the ability to enter previously prohibited activities like investment banking.

This consolidation-deregulation approach utterly ignores the causes of past crises, and fails to address the financial needs of most American households, businesses, or communities. It won't provide the capital that banks need or the credit that customers aren't getting. And it offers no new moral framework or contract between the industry and the citizenry that so handsomely subsidizes it by establishing public obligations in return for the public guarantee of bank deposits.

In short, we have been talking about giving an overeater still another free lunch, thanks to the stranglehold that the powerful banking industry has over the Presidency, Congress, the Federal Reserve Board, the state legislatures, and much of the press.

But economic power isn't the same thing as wisdom, and we may still pursue a path toward a financial system that would channel the country's capital to the businesses, individuals, and neighborhoods that could most productively use it.

What follows are some of the ways in which we might construct such a money system.

LOAN, BABY, LOAN

During several hot summers in the 1960s, angry mobs of black rioters ran amok in the ghettos of Los Angeles, Newark, Detroit, and other American cities. As they torched the shops and stores of their neighborhoods, their cry was "Burn, baby, burn." Now we have seen their likes again, along with the sickening plumes of smoke, the bombed-out businesses, the violent made-for-TV mayhem. One person you have never seen charging through the streets, however, is someone with a shop or a home of his own.

How can more of the residents of our inner cities acquire that something of their own to protect, that piece of private property that turns them into a builder and defender of a neighborhood instead of its despoiler?

One group with an answer is ACORN, a twenty-three-year-old community-activist organization with a vision of civic responsibility that has changed the behavior of high public officials, once alienated slum dwellers, and conservative bankers alike. ACORN's secret is its willingness to go to the mat with a nonviolent kind of trouble it calls "body power": the only kind of power its minority members have. It is not to be confused with good manners.

All through the long, dry eighties, scores of community groups labored to stem the decline of poor neighborhoods despite the withering away of assistance from the federal government. ACORN was one of the most successful in renovating slum housing and in pressuring banks to make mortgage loans to low- and moderate-income borrowers. More recently, ACORN's successes are multiplying, thanks in part to the little-known Community Reinvestment Act, passed in 1977, which requires lenders "to meet the credit needs of the local communities in which they are chartered."

If a review of lending records finds that a bank has been redlining—that is, avoiding certain neighborhoods—the bank regulators are supposed to use their persuasive powers to remedy the bank's performance; as a last resort, regulators can deny branching, merger, or acquisition applications if compliance is not forthcoming.

Had it done what it was intended to do, this reasonable requirement of civic responsibility could have brought about a dramatically more equitable distribution of this country's capital in the last decade. By requiring banks to lend to local entrepreneurs and home buyers, it might have slowed the stampede of funds into Argentinean state monopolies, Brazilian boondoggles, leveraged buyouts, real estate shell games, and all the other glamorous sinkholes that banks poured their money into during what ought to be called the "dodo" years. The Community Reinvestment Act might even have prevented the S&L "debacle," a term that with its hint of natural disaster hides the fact that a lot of banksters were just plain reckless or dumb or crooked, or all of the above.

At first, the CRA did change a few things. By 1980, three

banks had had their branching or merger applications denied outright. More important, dozens of "Affirmative Lending Agreements" between banks and community organizations were signed, enjoining banks to make mortgage money available to needy neighborhoods and to invest in low- to moderate-income housing. A few watchdog groups sprang up to monitor local banks.

But the banks soon learned ways of wiggling around the law, and during the Reagan administration, the entire reform effort went into eclipse.

The law remained on the books, however, and when commercial banks began to apply for permission to merge in the mid-1980s, community groups had the tool they needed to challenge the mergers of banks that were not in compliance.

Enter ACORN. Founded in Little Rock, Arkansas, the non-profit neighborhood advocacy group is now a national organization with some seventy thousand members, most of them in households whose earnings range from $14,000 to $20,000. Their annual dues of $24 and some foundation money support a yearly budget of $3 million and offices in Little Rock; Brooklyn, New York; Philadelphia; New Orleans; and Washington, D.C.; among other cities.

By threatening to use banks' noncompliance with the CRA to challenge the megamergers, ACORN has pried loose an avalanche of loans for affordable housing. In so doing, they are proving again the fundamental lesson of the New Deal: Expanding capitalism and broadening its base can only strengthen the system.

The banks that have been pushed, kicking and screaming, into low-income mortgage lending are also finding, to their surprise, that there is money to be made. Well-run programs can break even in the short run and hold out the promise of substantial long-run gains. As poor neighborhoods stabilize, an entire area benefits, with a positive effect on banks' profitability.

Moreover, about 60 percent of American households have incomes of less than $25,000. This is a huge market that has gone completely untapped—which is another way of saying that many if not most Americans have not been served by the banking system. With commercial real estate dead, the oil patch depressed, big corporate borrowers gone for good, and foreign borrowers still crawling out of bad debts, maybe some banks will decide that ordinary Americans are not such a bad bet after all.

Like many nonprofit community organizations, ACORN has set up housing-development corporations to acquire fore-closed homes for resale. Typically, ACORN retains title to the ground through a land trust and sells the house to a buyer who must put in money and "sweat equity," that is, time spent rehabilitating the dwelling.

This basic model has created approximately five hundred homes for homesteading families all around the country. By late 1991, ACORN housing corporations were rehabilitating or had in the pipeline almost three hundred more homes na-tionwide.

The group also led a successful effort to persuade Congress to establish a program within the Resolution Trust Corpo-ration to make moderately priced houses acquired from bank insolvencies available to low-income families. Angered by the RTC's foot-dragging on home sales to low-income buyers, ACORN fell back on body power again, squatting in RTC houses, staging sit-ins in RTC offices, lobbying Congress, and, finally, suing.

It worked. The RTC was ultimately mandated to establish a program that has resulted in the sale of more than twenty thousand homes to low-income buyers. To this extent, the

RTC has actually done a better job than the Department of Housing and Urban Development, which is selling thousands of vacant foreclosed homes to the highest bidder, despite HUD secretary Jack Kemp's rhetoric about encouraging low-income home ownership.

But government housing is nothing compared to the vast amounts of private capital that could be made available to low-income and minority borrowers. A 1991 Federal Reserve study of five million mortgage applications showed that blacks were turned down twice as frequently as whites, even at the same income levels, a pattern of discrimination that has also been documented by numerous other studies over the past few years. ACORN's greatest achievement may be its current effort to use the CRA to restructure the country's private mortgage-lending system.

Since 1985, at least twenty-nine banks have been persuaded to put more than $500 million into inner-city housing, financing some sixteen thousand mortgages. The typical borrower earns $10,000 to $25,000 a year and obtains a mortgage, usually in the $20,000-to-$30,000 range, at slightly below-market rates.

And that is just the beginning. After ACORN threatened to challenge their mergers, several of the country's largest banks have decided to comply with the reinvestment law. The Chemical Banking Corporation, formed after a merger with Manufacturers Hanover Corporation, has pledged $750 million for inner-city mortgages in New York. And NationsBank, the goliath created by the merger of the NCNB Corporation and the C&S/Sovran Bank, has committed itself to lend as much as *$10 billion* for low-income mortgages, residential rehabilitation, and multifamily housing projects.

This kind of money can begin to reverse the deterioration of poor neighborhoods into drug-infested slums and change the very quality of urban life. For when banks won't lend in a neighborhood, the only house sales are to people who can pay cash or a big down payment. And only two kinds of people can do that: drug dealers and absentee landlords.

None of this happened without frequent acrimonious meetings between bank executives and ACORN representatives, and industry resistance has been fierce. In 1991, the powerful banking lobby came close to giving the Community Reinvestment Act the coup de grace by slipping into banking legislation a provision that would have exempted small, local banks (80 to 90 percent of the industry) from the law.

ACORN rode to the rescue. Busloads of activists poured into Washington, picketed the offices of the Independent Bankers Association of America with bullhorns and banners, and camped out overnight in front of the Rayburn House Office Building in order to guarantee themselves seats in the hearing room for the vote on the proposed legislation. When the minions of finance arrived the next morning, they found themselves stuck out in the hall. The Banking Committee voted down the bankers' proposal by a decisive majority.

Over the years, banks have excused their failure to lend in poorer neighborhoods on the grounds that deals involving land trusts, "sweat equity," and unconventional borrowers are not accepted by the secondary buyers of mortgages, Fannie Mae (the Federal National Mortgage Association) and Freddie Mac (the Federal Home Loan Mortgage Company). These agencies purchase mortgages that meet their standards and then pool them into securities for sale to investors. The secondary markets reduce banks' risks and free up bank capital for more lending.

According to figures released by the Federal Reserve Board, only 19.3 percent of Freddie Mac's business and 19.1 percent of Fannie Mae's served lower-income people and areas. The restrictive underwriting criteria used by the two agencies have thus inadvertently encouraged banks to discriminate against minority and low-income borrowers and inner-city neighborhoods.

In a series of heated meetings, ACORN began in 1989 to challenge the agencies' policies. By the summer of 1991, Freddie Mac and Fannie Mae had agreed to negotiate. Eventually, the agencies agreed to buy $1.75 billion a year in "nonconforming" mortgages.

The deal was ultimately codified into tough legislation that, as of this writing, will require the two agencies to direct 30 percent of their mortgage purchases to low- and median-income borrowers and to those living in mortgage-credit-starved areas. That translates into more than *$70 billion* in mortgage capital each year. No enterprise zones, no micro-loans, no *nothing*, could make such a difference to the quality of life in America's inner cities.

And the passage of this legislation occurred only because a group of poor activists, about as far outside the established system as one can get, decided to change the way things work.

BANKING AS IF PEOPLE MATTERED

The latest wave of bank failures and mergers is producing an increasing concentration of ownership and control of banking resources. The trend worries populists, who get nervous when too much financial power is held in a few hands—can political power be far behind? Besides, megabanks have very poor track records in lending to people and communities who really need the money.

Take South Central Los Angeles, the scene of the worst domestic riots in decades, riots that are going to cost taxpayers hundreds of millions of dollars in "disaster relief." In a recent investigation of redlining, a coalition called Communities for Accountable Reinvestment found that during a fourteen-month period in 1987 and 1988, giant BankAmerica made only one of the thirteen single-family home loans granted to borrowers in South Central L.A., a community of 500,000 people. The second-largest California bank, Security Pacific, made three loans.

Meanwhile, deposits at the twelve BankAmerica and Security Pacific branches in South Central grew thirteen times faster than the banks' statewide deposits, from $323 million in midyear 1987 to $408 million in midyear 1989 (one does wonder where all that money came from—the booming eighties were apparently better for some poor neighborhoods than we commonly think).

Despite their dismal lending record, the two banks (now merged into a single $190 billion institution) won high marks from the tolerant government enforcers of the Community Reinvestment Act. A dozen other Los Angeles lenders flunked, comprising a fifth of all U.S. banks failing to meet the CRA test of investing in their home communities.

With little access to the banking system, poor borrowers have to turn to usurers for credit. South Central L.A. has only nineteen bank and S&L branches. According to the study by Communities for Accountable Reinvestment, 54 percent of all single-family home mortgages in the area from 1987 to 1989 were written by mortgage and finance companies, which usually charge sky-high rates.

As one banking expert in Washington told me, "Communities [like South Central] don't need tax breaks and enterprise zones. They need *financing*."

CHARLIE MAC
The Securities and Exchange Commission was expected, as of this writing, to modify rules that restrict loans backed by receivables as a means of steering more credit to enterprises.

An even more sophisticated step would be to establish a secondary mortgage agency, similar to Fannie Mae and Freddie Mac, for small-business loans in communities where credit is scarce. We could call it Charlie Mac—the Commercial Enterprise Mortgage Association.

Charlie Mac could pick up loans originated by conventional banks, credit unions, and community-development banks and made in areas with below-median income profiles. Establishing such an institution *would* shift the risk of such lending from private companies to the public, but the benefits are probably great enough to justify the public subsidy involved. Banking experts at all frequencies of the political spectrum agree that the idea would do more to revitalize needful neighborhoods than a hundred enterprise zones—and would cost the Treasury much less.

PUBLIC-PURPOSE BANKS

The existence of a Charlie Mac would help stimulate the development of many more community-oriented credit unions and depositor-owned development banks. The Financial Democracy Campaign has long been advocating an expansion of the ranks of such "public-purpose banks."

A national network of democratically owned lenders could also be created out of the ruined banks and thrifts now held by the Resolution Trust Corporation and the Federal Deposit Insurance Corporation, and from the required divestitures of branches by merging banks. These franchises could be given or sold on a preferential basis to existing community-development banks, loan funds, credit unions, and other "good guy" lenders. Where no such development banks exist, the franchises could be newly chartered as depositor-owned institutions.

State and local governments and pension funds could provide some of these public-purpose banks' initial capital, and a small portion of the transaction deposits of public agencies could be required to be deposited in the new banks. In turn, the banks would be required to do the vast bulk of their lending in priority areas including local housing, community and industrial development, health and child-care activities, and environmental protection. Call them the lemonade banks, made from the lemons of the S&L debacle.

A LENDERS' CORPS

Another pet idea of the Financial Democracy Campaign is to provide new and existing community-based lenders with modest retraining funds to enable them to hire some of the hundreds of thousands of people who lost their jobs in banking and finance during the 1980s—an unemployment bloodbath that has received far less media attention than the loss of jobs in the blue-collar trades. These experienced people could bring needed technical and managerial expertise to public-purpose banks.

Some have also suggested that we restore the historic mission of the S&L industry, which was to provide broad community housing assistance. Thrifts could be required to invest at least 30 percent of their cash in local community development and housing for low- and moderate-income families, and to hold a high proportion of their assets in mortgages for properties within a fifty-mile radius of the lending branch. To prevent them from straying too far from this mandate, states wouldn't be able to allow thrifts to enter businesses beyond those allowed by the federal government.

A CENTRAL BANK FOR COMMUNITY LENDERS

Another proposal would transform the Federal Home Loan Bank system into a central bank for community lenders.

The FHLB system certainly does need a new mission. At the moment, it is a public source of capital without much to do. The regional Home Loan Banks are authorized to borrow in the long-term credit markets at a government-subsidized rate and then lend the money to S&Ls, which in turn lend to the public at a reduced rate. The banks charge the S&Ls a small spread, which constitutes the system's profit.

But now that the FHLB system's clientele is moribund, financial reformers argue that it should begin to lend to community institutions that finance low-income and multifamily housing, homeless shelters, small businesses, and the like—meeting the critical, long-term credit needs of those whom the banking system has never served.

Since 1989, the FHLB system, per the terms of the first S&L bailout legislation, has had to place $100 million a year into a special pool for low-income mortgages. ACORN and other advocates want to expand that initiative into a reform of the entire system. They would require that 10 percent of the assets of each Home Loan Bank be set aside for community and housing loans specifically targeted to families with incomes 80 percent or more below the median level.

Critics argue that these loans would be risky and would jeopardize the stability of the FHLB system. One can only reply, More risky than what? And what stability are we talking about? Of the S&L's? Of our inner cities? As it was previously incarnated, the FHLB system is all but dead, buried under the failures of "conventional" banking. If a nationwide community-banking system existed, we might have more stability in our poor neighborhoods than most of us can remember.

TIGHTEN THE LID ON THE COOKIE JAR

There is no sense talking about a new kind of financial system if we don't install some real wrist slappers for the hands in the cookie jar. A pair of suggestions:

- All members and employees of the House and Senate banking committees, officials of the bank regulatory agencies, and top White House and Cabinet officials should be banned from having anything to do with the banking business for at least five years after leaving government.

- The punishment for financial crimes should be dramatically increased. As folk singer Woody Guthrie said, "More people have suffered from the point of a fountain pen than from a gun." (California judge Lance A. Ito quoted this bit of populist wisdom when he sentenced Charles H. Keating, Jr., to ten years in the slammer for defrauding S&L customers out of millions of dollars.)

I like the idea of confiscatory fines—stripping malefactors above a certain level of larceny of their personal assets—and imaginative sentences like community service in homeless shelters and drug-abuse clinics.

Big-time financial crooks could also be put to work using their obvious talents. For every dollar they are able to raise for nonprofit community organizations and charities, they might have some time chopped off their sentence.

NO MORE BANK BAILOUTS: HOW TO REFORM DEPOSIT INSURANCE

Any real reform in the finance industry would have to attend to the breakdown of distinctions among banks and securities firms, mutual funds, and the commercial paper market. When the commercial banks say that they want a "level playing field" with all of these nonbank competitors, they mean that they want to be freed of the regulations that the others are not subject to.

The banks have a point, but the answer is not to lower the standards of the game but to raise them—to put the financial playing field on higher ground.

All companies engaged in the financial business should operate under uniform regulation, meeting capital, reserve, liquidity, disclosure, and diversification requirements similar to those now imposed on banks. Not only would this enhance the stability of the system, it would enable the Federal Reserve to apply monetary policy, currently the government's principal tool in influencing overall economic activity, much more broadly and effectively. That is no small gain.

Further, the deposit insurance system should be radically changed so that it protects *depositors* rather than *institutions*. The point is to insure individuals' savings (up to a set amount) and organizations' transactions accounts wherever they are: in the banks, thrifts, credit unions, mutual funds, and pension plans governed by the Employee Retirement Income Security Act, where the bulk of small savers' funds are deposited.

The safety of the insurance arrangements of some of these fiduciaries has yet to be tested by a major crisis. It is especially troubling that transactions (checking) accounts of businesses, nonprofits, and governments—all the monies required to meet payrolls, pay for purchases, and so on—are not covered by the current $100,000 protection policy, as some poor communities have found out to their dismay. Those kinds of accounts need to be 100 percent insured.

But how could all this expanded insurance be paid for? Taxpayers are already exposed to a contingent liability of some $3 trillion (the total amount of all deposits held in U.S. banks, thrifts, and credit unions). If other federal financial guarantees and credit programs are taken into account, the public is already on the hook for $5 trillion in potential losses.

According to one proposal, depositors would pay the cost of their own insurance. Individuals would be required to purchase financial-guarantee insurance to cover their savings, up to a set amount. They would do this by accepting a lower rate of interest on insured deposits, with the difference—the premium—deducted by the savings institution and paid directly into an insurance fund. The individual's premium would be tax deductible. The system would allow for some flexibility: The amount insured could vary with the size of the household, and small savers could be exempt from or pay lower premiums.

Such a plan would cover savings in all federally regulated institutions, and would include all state and local pension plans as well as assets held by insurance companies. (Insurance companies now manage one third of the nation's pension assets, offer other savings vehicles for small savers, and are the primary providers for the nation's health-insurance system. The industry is dominated by a number of large companies that operate nationwide, but the quality of state regulation, which is all there is, varies, and the soundness of the state guarantee funds is highly suspect. Some observers see insurance as the next big time bomb in the financial system. National regulation is one reform that probably shouldn't wait.)

The transactions balances of businesses and governments would also be fully insured but would not be paid *any* interest. Banks could take a fixed profit on the earnings from these noninterest-bearing demand deposits and pay the remainder into the insurance fund. This stable income would improve the banks' profitability and maybe even encourage them to reduce some of the exorbitant fees they are now charging the rest of us.

One of the objections to this reform is that it would be difficult to administer. Individuals could place their money in a variety of institutions to get around the limits on insurance. But if the IRS can track down tax cheaters, it can probably find a way to detect deposit insurance cheaters as well.

· IX ·

A New Deal for Small Companies

FILLING THE CAPITAL GAP

Without creating new bureaucracies, spending taxpayers' money, or using undue coercion, state and local governments have found a myriad innovative ways to persuade banks to lend to small companies. Once we have real economic leadership in the White House, the federal government could promote these ideas all over the country.

Boston, for instance, is simply using the attraction of city deposits to encourage banks to lend more to enterprises in minority neighborhoods and for home mortgages. In 1989, the city began asking banks to disclose information about lending practices, then graded their performance in lending to poor areas and adjusted its deposits accordingly. Some banks were rewarded and some saw their city deposits walk out the door. According to the minority-owned Boston Bank of Commerce, the city's pressure has made other banks realize that they can actually make money in parts of the city they had given up on.

Another imaginative program has been devised by the Michigan Strategic Fund, a development-finance institution set up in the mid-1980s as part of an effort to help the stricken state economy adjust to a massive loss of manufacturing jobs.

The MSF has been working specifically toward stimulating the flow of capital to new and early-stage businesses, and has had much success, using a simple, cost-effective concept that deserves to become a national model.

The MSF "capital access" program works like portfolio insurance. A special reserve fund is set up for each participating bank, earmarked to cover losses on loans within the program. Each borrower pays a one-time premium charge into the reserve of 1.5 to 3.5 percent of the total loan, which charge is matched by a bank premium payment. The state then matches the combined total. If a loss occurs, the full reserve amount is available to cover it.

In its first five years—through 1991—more than $65 million was loaned under the MSF's "capital access" program to some fifteen hundred small businesses, most of them distinctly "nonbankable" companies—more than 90 percent have sales of less than $1 million; 60 percent have sales of less than $200,000; 20 percent were start-ups. Many of the loans were made to companies that had been turned down by the SBA; the MSF's average loan—about $50,000—is much smaller than the typical SBA loan.

The program, in other words, is doing what it was intended to do—steer money to firms that weren't being served by the capital markets or by the federal government's small-business lending program. And it is accomplishing this at a minimal cost to the public. Only $3.1 million of state money has been put into the program, which means that the state is getting a twenty-to-one leverage on its investment. And the entire program has been managed for the most part by a single professional staff person.

No subsidies are given to the borrowers, who pay strictly market rates or, because of the premium, even slightly more. Loss rates so far are running at about 4.5 percent, higher than normal but well within a manageable range.

"It's the wave of the future," says Steven Rohde, who designed the program. "The banks love it—it gives them a new marketing tool. The companies love it—it's a great leverage of public resources. And it can have bipartisan support—it transcends ideology."

According to Rohde, West Virginia has allocated funds for a capital-access program, Oklahoma has approved a fund, and Utah, Oregon, and Indiana are working on similar programs. New York City in the summer of 1992 established a $5 million Small Business Reserve Fund based on the Michigan initiative. There is no reason why the idea couldn't be implemented on a national scale, as one response to the persistent failure of the banking system to lend to credit-pressed small companies.

Says Rohde, describing what has been termed the "new paradigm": "We have some long-term structural issues we need to address in the economy. This approach uses government initiative to find a private-sector solution. It shows how we can use public resources to help the private sector be more effective."

AN INDUSTRIAL-EXTENSION SERVICE

Ralph Nader thinks that we have so many problems because the most important things are boring.

It's boring enough to talk about ways of revitalizing American industry but even worse to get into details, like how to adopt computer-aided design, computer-controlled manufacturing systems, just-in-time inventory management, or statistical-process control. Small and midsized American manufacturing companies have been slow to adapt to these modern ways of doing things—slower than their Japanese and European rivals. And since innovation is the key to lower cost production, this technological reluctance could mean a steady loss of business and jobs to faster-footed firms overseas.

Earlier American entrepreneurs understood the importance of constant innovation. Andrew Carnegie scrapped virtually new plants when he learned of cheaper methods of making steel, leaving his British competition and their older equipment in the dust. And Henry Ford once observed that he might as well buy the latest machinery, because if he didn't, he'd have to pay for it anyway—in lost sales.

In the United States today, there are about 355,000 smaller manufacturing firms (defined as those with fewer than five hundred employees). They produce more than one half of all value-added in manufacturing and directly employ more than eight million people. So their need to stay on top of the latest technology is crucial to economic growth.

One way to accomplish this is by establishing an industrial-extension service, loosely modeled on the agricultural-extension service that, since 1914, has been transferring research developed in universities and USDA laboratories to individual farmers. The system enabled American farmers to overtake their European competitors in farming techniques and to become the most productive in the world. Today, the program has an annual budget of $1.1 billion and a staff of sixteen thousand people (including one extension worker for every 150 or so farmers)—for a sector that contributes less than 2 percent of our GDP.

No one argues that this model should be replicated, if only because creating vast new bureaucracies is not the name of the game anymore. But something *like* an extension service might be just the thing in manufacturing, which has been relatively starved for government attention. A recent study calculated that direct and indirect federal support for industrial extension and technology transfer amounts to less than $25 million a year—this in service of a sector that accounts for roughly 16 percent of the U.S. GDP.

Ironically, the industrial-extension idea was adopted in Japan in the late 1940s, largely at the urging of the New Dealers who helped run the Occupation. The Japanese Robotics Association, for example, searches the world for new ideas, translates the material into Japanese, and sends people out to assist member companies. The government, meanwhile, allows quick write-offs on new robotics as an incentive for companies to use the most modern equipment.

Altogether, Japan spends $500 million a year on industrial extension and technology. Experts suggest that the federal government could reach about half of U.S. manufacturing firms in a five-year period by spending $75 million to $125 million a year, such funds to be matched by the states. Some twenty-three state governments already support technology-extension centers, but the best state industrial-extension programs usually help no more than a few hundred firms a year. An expansion of their efforts could begin to correct U.S. companies' relative backwardness in product-development methods, design, quality control, shop-floor organization, inventory management, and work-force training.

To the extent that the federal government has entered the picture, largely through the National Institute of Standards and Technology, it has favored the establishment of regional centers for the transfer of more charismatic, state-of-the-art, government-developed technology. These efforts tend to be directed toward larger firms, and involve expensive, sophisticated technologies that most smaller firms cannot absorb. Similarly, the more than $40 billion in the Defense Department's massive R&D budget includes almost $500 million for technology transfer. Most of that is for the fancy stuff, not for the kind of process technology that smaller firms need.

Why not put that $500 million, or even half of it, into a plain old vanilla industrial-extension service, supplemented by workshops, demonstrations, and technical publications? None of this is glamorous or even particularly high-tech work, which harks back to Ralph Nader's point. But it's better to be boring than to be left behind.

COMPANY NETWORKING

The second idea on how to revitalize the key small-business sector is really an old idea, going back to the artisans' guilds of Renaissance Italy. The current term for it is *networking*: smaller firms joining together in cooperative arrangements to introduce new technologies and share information. For example, the Italian Confederazione Nazionale Dell'Artigianato assists small firms with fewer than twenty employees in financing, training, design, and marketing, and similar examples of collaboration can be found in Sweden and Germany, in New York's garment district, and around the film industry in southern California. (Networking is easier if small enterprises in the same industry are clustered geographically.)

Denmark has had particular and noteworthy networking success. In 1988, the country faced a large and growing trade deficit, high unemployment, and low investment. The Ministry of Trade and Industry commissioned a study by an American consulting firm, whose report concluded that Denmark's fundamental problem was that its companies were too small to compete. But a few months later, C. Richard Hatch of the New Jersey Institute of Technology told a group of Danish officials and businessmen that the problem wasn't size, but competence. Based on what he had observed of Italian small-business networks whose success had helped Italy overtake France as the world's fourth-biggest manufacturing economy, Hatch argued that such associations might work for Denmark.

Within eighteen months, more than 3000 of Denmark's 7300 manufacturing companies were actively involved in networks, cooperating in marketing, the joint use of advanced technology, product development, and quality control. Approximately $25 million in government funds had helped launch the associations by doing feasibility studies and covering some early costs. (Nonetheless, Hatch asserts that it isn't always necessary for the public to invest in these kinds of plans. If they make sense, he says, business will find a way to make them happen; the real purpose of initial public support is to get large numbers of firms to think seriously about cooperation.)

In the United States, networks have sprung up in certain industries (woodworking, metalworking, forging) dominated by small, vulnerable firms. For the most part, however, American trade associations focus on lobbying Washington or the state capitals for favorable legislation rather than trying to help their members gain strength through cooperation.

Advocates of networking insist that the antitrust laws do not pose a problem for associations sharing marketing and export ideas, designing training programs, and other vital business-support activities. The real problem is the cowboy mentality of so much of American business, to which cooperation is simply a foreign idea. As we have found elsewhere, at the root of an economic problem is an attitude problem: a cultural resistance to communal action. But this me-against-them, them-against-us view of the world is impoverishing us all.

Certainly, other nations understand the power of a communitarian outlook. It has been pointed out that one reason why smaller firms in Japan can invest in new technology is the long-term, stable relationships they maintain with their large corporate customers. This "relational contracting" contrasts with the "spot contracting" more common in the United

States, where uncertainty over where the next order is coming from makes it hard for small firms to invest in new technology.

The paradoxical conclusion: Small American manufacturers can become far more competitive globally if they can learn to be more cooperative at home.

· X ·

Housing: How to Put a Roof over Every Head

Nothing has disturbed the social conscience of the country as much as the pervasive problem of the homeless.

Foreign visitors are shocked at the sight of homeless people sleeping over sewer grates in the nation's capital, begging outside the door of suburban drugstores, staking out sidewalks outside office towers in all our big cities. In New York City, the subways and train stations look like scenes out of Brueghel—or India. (I traveled on the Indian subcontinent for a few months in the early 1970s. It was inconceivable to an American then that the sight of homeless families curled up in drainage pipes in Bombay or lined up for their daily meal outside a mission in Calcutta was a precursor of similar sights fifteen years later in the United States.)

The very visibility of the homeless has been a major contributor to the sense of hopelessness so many Americans feel in the face of social problems. Their presence personifies all our fears that our own situation is precarious and seems to confirm that we are becoming a Third World nation that can't even take care of its people's most basic needs.

It is important to understand that a "what can we do?" despair over the homeless is nonsense. This tragedy is no act of God. More than anything else, it is a direct consequence of falling wages and a shrinkage in the supply of housing that poor people can afford. Throw in the absence of a national health policy that would provide adequate care for the mentally ill, many of whom are on the streets, a 70 percent reduction in federally subsidized housing programs during the 1980s, an economic recession, and a drug epidemic, and you have it—a crisis.

Today, there are approximately 7 million households that cannot afford housing without some kind of assistance. Housing advocates believe that it would take roughly $15 billion to $19 billion—roughly twice what we are now spending on low-income housing needs—to provide housing assistance to everyone in America who needs it.

That is serious money, but not out of the question. In fact, we are spending just about the same amount of public money subsidizing the houses of the wealthiest Americans. If we really want to end the housing crisis, all we have to do is shift that subsidy to the needy. Simple.

THE JACUZZI SUBSIDY

If the nation's housing were reducible to the blueprint of a fancy home, here's how we could fix our present crisis: We'd just eliminate those his-and-her spa bathrooms and put on a dormitory addition. Final additional construction cost: zero.

■ ■ ■

Of the estimated $100 billion the federal government spends on housing every year, only "a tiny pot of subsidies" goes into low-income housing, according to C. Austin Fitts, who headed the Federal Housing Administration during the early years of the Bush administration. The rest goes to surprisingly well off homeowners.

Here are some eyebrow-raising numbers:

- Roughly half the $69 billion in homeowner tax deductions goes to people with incomes of more than $75,000 a year.
- Those with incomes below $40,000 (79 percent of taxpayers) received only 19.2 percent of the tax break.
- The percentage of middle-class taxpayers (those with incomes between $30,000 and $40,000) who claimed the mortgage deduction is down to less than 40 percent.
- Since wealthy taxpayers pay a 31 percent income tax, 31 percent of their mortgage-interest payments are subsidized by the government—twice the rate of subsidy enjoyed by those in the lowest tax bracket of 15 percent. If the mortgage-interest tax deduction were capped at 15 percent for just the wealthiest 2 percent of homeowners—those with incomes of more than $150,000—the government would save $15 billion a year!

We might call this eliminating the Jacuzzi subsidy.

If we did that one thing, we would generate enough money to provide housing assistance to almost everyone who needs it. Such a redistribution of official favors from rich to poor could change the quality of life in this country.

It is hard to imagine a more painless way to accomplish a giant leap in our national well-being. The myth that our housing and deficit problems are so great that we can do nothing about them is just that—a complete myth. At the moment, Donald Trump gets a deduction on every one of his homes, and a poor single mother who loses her rented apartment gets none. By any measure of a civilized society, that ain't fair.

It's not good economics, either. Observers have often noted that because of the huge tax subsidies for housing in the United States, an unnaturally inflated amount of savings is directed into real estate rather than into other, potentially more productive investments. Generous tax write-offs and the relatively low down payment required to buy a house in the United States also encourage what economists call "dissavings," the accumulation of debt. In Germany, buyers typically have to put down 40 percent of the price of a house; in Italy, as much as 50 percent. A number of economists would raise down-payment requirements in the United States in order to encourage more productive saving habits.

Touching the mortgage-interest deduction may be the political equivalent of kissing a red-hot poker, but the number of studies recently devoted to the issue indicates that a change may be in the wind. A proposal to limit deductions on mortgage interest to the first $250,000 on a mortgage was in Ross Perot's economic plan; who knows where a similar suggestion will turn up next.

IN LAND WE TRUST

The Indians never understood, to their ultimate sorrow, the white man's notion that an individual could own the world we live in. The idea of appropriating the sky or the water or the land for one's own private purposes was simply incomprehensible.

In the 1960s, the Indian concept was revived by environmentalists as a way of restoring a sense of stewardship of the land, and the practice of setting undeveloped land aside in a conservation trust has since become quite common.

Now, the housing crisis has brought another kind of land trust to the fore—one that provides permanent housing affordability by removing land from the speculative real estate market.

More than one hundred community land trusts have sprung up in twenty-three states around the country. All operate in more or less the same way: A nonprofit open-membership community organization acquires land and either rents or leases the housing on it to low- and moderate-income families.

Because the cost of the land is removed from the price of the housing, home prices can be lowered by as much as one third. And though the purchasers can transfer the house to their heirs, who can renew the lease, or sell it outright, their gain will be limited to the rate of inflation plus the value of any reasonable improvements. The community trust keeps the housing under a form of price control: It remains affordable virtually forever.

The land-trust concept was inspired in part by a similar movement initiated in India in the 1950s, a voluntary land-reform effort to create "village trusts" to hold land for landless farmers.

As one advocate put it, "Since no human effort created land, it's unfair for human beings to profit from the sale of land." But it's perhaps more realistic to say that land trusts are a growing trend in housing because they can deliver the goods for communities that are in dire need of reasonably priced homes.

They are found in places like Washington State's San Juan Islands, where wealthy retirees and vacationers drove the price of real estate up 47 percent between 1989 and 1990, making the beautiful islands too expensive for local working people to live on. They are taking hold in Maine, where paper companies own 80 percent of the land and out-of-state residents have pushed land values and property taxes beyond the reach of many locals. They are spreading in central Massachusetts, where an average single-family home that cost $38,900 in 1980 now costs $100,000. A two-bedroom house in the same area, owned by a land trust, rents for $389 a month. And they work on New York City's Lower East Side, where poor homesteaders use sweat equity to renovate abandoned, addict-infested, dilapidated buildings and then rent two-bedroom apartments for $400 a month, thanks to a land trust called RAIN—Rehabilitation in Action to Improve Neighborhoods.

Federal support of low-income housing should include matching grants to well-established land trusts. The community trusts can give the public much more bang for its buck than endless rent subsidies—just as buying a house is almost always smarter than renting. Once property is acquired and set aside, the housing becomes a permanent part of the affordable stock, and each successive owner or renter will reap the benefits without using any additional public money. After an initial investment, the government is out of it—unlike government-owned public housing or government rent subsidies to private landlords.

Up to now, community land trusts have relied mostly on foundation and church money, although some cities and state pension funds have kicked in to help finance real estate purchases.

Why not offer a greater portion of federal housing assistance as seed money, or matching grants, to the many community-housing associations and local government programs that have sprung up over the past few years, for the acquisition, rehabilitation, and construction of decent housing for the poor? These groups have established a track record of building and operating affordable housing far more efficiently and inexpensively than either the federal government or the private sector. All they lack is something only the federal government can provide—a truly useful sum of money.

· XI ·

Consumer
Power

THE POWER OF ORGANIZED PEOPLE

As someone once said, "There are two kinds of power: organized money and organized people."

The case for independent, broad-based economic organizations rests not just on appeals to fairness and the right of all to be heard. The truth is, with regulation co-opted by the regulated industries themselves, citizens' groups are about all that's left as a check on unrestrained corporate statism.

Imagine, for example, what might have happened if a strong consumer group, reflecting the antinuclear sentiments of much of the public, had been able to block the construction of nuclear power plants back in the 1970s. The industry would have been saved from throwing $265 billion into a massively misplaced investment that "only the blind, or the biased," as *Forbes* magazine put it in 1985, could think was money well spent.

Or what if consumers had been able to tell the S&Ls, "No, you cannot run off and buy real estate in faraway places you know nothing about"? How dreadful could the consequences have been, compared to what happened?

And what if a powerful consumer group now had the clout to tell health-insurance companies that they must insure everyone who can pay a reasonable premium? We might not be discussing the possibility of bypassing the private companies in favor of a single national insurer.

If the government won't save regulated industries from themselves, maybe the public can. The economy can't afford *not* to have greater citizen advocacy and empowerment.

One suggestion is a federal funding law, similar to the law that matches campaign monies for serious presidential candidates, for any consumer-advocacy group that meets certain criteria, such as open membership and a nonpartisan regulatory or monitoring purpose.

Something like this already exists on the state level in intervenor-compensation programs, which make funds available to qualified consumer groups that represent interests not otherwise advocated in regulatory proceedings.

The law should also make it easier for public-interest groups to build up their membership, allowing them to place their literature in all public buildings and granting them franking privileges and/or access to selected government mailings, like those from the IRS.

"Electronic town meetings" at which the public can register its views are fine, but people can't just sit on the couch in the splendid isolation of their homes and expect to wield any real power. Those who want power must join organizations that can research their case and carry their voice into civic meetings, boardrooms, and the halls of government. The only way that harried private citizens can achieve any influence is by acting in concert with others. (And even then, they may have to take to the streets now and then, so hard has it become for ordinary citizens to influence the political process.)

CITIZEN UTILITY BOARDS

Citizen utility boards are one of the best examples of popular economic organizations in the country today. They don't cost the taxpayers any money. They don't challenge the political rights of any other interest group. They simply write into the script those who have been left out: the general public.

CUBs represent residential ratepayers in regulatory proceedings before legislatures and in the courts, often with amazing success. The largest CUB, in Illinois, has more than 100,000 dues-paying members; its supporters claim that it has saved the state's taxpayers as much as $3 billion since its inception in 1984. Among other things, the group won a revision of the state's Public Utilities Act, mandating that utilities use the least-expensive power available, and it forced several rollbacks of Commonwealth Edison rate increases, winning substantial refunds for consumers.

In San Diego, California, the San Diego Gas & Electric Company's rates have dropped 47 percent since the mid-1980s, due in large part to the Utility Consumers Action Network's championing of cheaper power purchases. UCAN was also part of a coalition that in 1991 successfully opposed a merger between San Diego Gas & Electric and Southern California Edison.

The CUB in Oregon focuses primarily on telephone issues. It has argued successfully for policies benefiting low-income consumers, such as the establishment of "lifeline" rates, and in 1990 calculated that it had fought for refunds and rate reductions totaling $124 million, a savings of $318 for every $1 spent.

The key to CUB success goes back to the early 1970s, when consumer activists were trying to figure out how to develop advocacy groups that would be free of both the political constraints plaguing government regulators and "public advocates" *and* the chronic funding problems of truly independent consumer groups. Ralph Nader came up with the idea of placing inserts into companies' billing envelopes and into mailings of all contracts, including leases, insurance policies, loan arrangements, and warranties. Such inserts would inform consumers of important issues and upcoming hearings, and solicit new members for consumer organizations, who could thus inexpensively piggyback their organizing and fund-raising onto existing mailings.

In 1980, the concept was first used in utility-company mailings to form a CUB in Wisconsin; three other states quickly followed. More CUBs were on the drawing board in New York, Massachusetts, Missouri, Kansas, and Florida when a Supreme Court decision in 1986 struck down on First Amendment grounds the use of bill inserts by consumer groups. The decision was a severe setback for the entire movement. The Illinois CUB lost one quarter of its membership in 1987 because it couldn't afford to solicit new members to replace those lost through attrition. But it was saved by state legislation allowing it to insert its messages into state mailings going to at least fifty thousand households. Two of these new mailings were particularly effective: the inserts into state income-tax refunds and license-plate renewals.

The Illinois CUB remains a champion in its field, urging members by direct mail and phone bank to write lawmakers and to attend rallies and "lobby days" in the state capital, where the organization maintains one full-time lobbyist. The CUB also runs a toll-free hot line to assist customers with billing problems and to disseminate information.

A FINANCIAL CONSUMERS' ASSOCIATION

The gays, the grays, the truckers, and just about everybody else is organized except those of us who go to the bank, put a little money in, and hope our checks don't bounce. It's just us, on our own, against the Desert Storm troopers of the banking lobby. That's why our children will be paying for the S&L mess for the rest of their lives. And that's why so many people were so upset by the checkbook scandals in Congress —the mess underlined the relative powerlessness of the rest of us when it comes to the money system.

How can we compete with a financial industry that between 1985 and 1991 gave members of Congress more than $36 million in campaign contributions through its political action committees?

Some two hundred lobbyists for the banks work the Congress—a number ascertained by counting up the motley crew in running shoes who line up outside hearing rooms before important hearings and votes, holding places for better-dressed guys who later breeze in from lunch at the Occidental Grill or La Colline to take their seats. There are maybe four full-time lobbyists in Washington for financial consumers' organizations.

And before we cry out against wicked Washington once again, note that things are no better in the state legislatures, which have their own "for sale" signs in the front yard. A survey of the legislative staff in five states, conducted by the Public Citizen's Congress Watch, found that consumer representation in state financial regulatory matters was virtually nonexistent.

What difference does it make?

Well, if you've ever wondered how the commercial banks are recovering from their decade-long orgy of bad lending, just look in the mirror.

You are earning less than 4 percent interest on your bank deposits, and if you hold a bank credit card, you are paying close to 20 percent interest, doing your bit to rebuild balance sheets ravaged by dumb loans to the Third World and flashy real estate developers.

Usury has made a comeback. Although half the states in this country limit or ban credit-card fees for late payments, credit overages, and annual renewals, banks charge them anyway, arguing that they are governed only by the laws in the states where their credit-card operations are based: Delaware and South Dakota. In 1991, banks collected $3.5 billion from their credit-card businesses, including an estimated $1.13 billion in penalties. When President Bush dared to suggest a federal law limiting exorbitant fees and interest rates on credit cards, bank stocks plummeted—that's the extent to which banks depend on us to make up for their past mistakes.

More than a dozen lawsuits are challenging the banks' violation of state usury laws, but in the meantime, there are things we can do to obtain interest-rate justice.

If you are a good customer and take the trouble to write and complain, your credit-card company may respond, quietly, by shaving off a couple of interest points on your account. But a far more effective solution would be to lobby for a nationwide Financial Consumers' Association, which could become "the silicon chip of the consumer movement," as Ralph Nader has put it. An FCA could even the odds in the finance game a little bit, giving the banks something closer to their own size to play around with. A consumers' group could monitor legislation and regulation involving all kinds of lenders, lobby for reforms, and publish useful consumer reports comparing banks' fees and services and alerting the public to gouging or discriminatory practices. It could also issue red alerts on redlining and mobilize consumers for brown-bag lunches with legislative staff and journalists (who don't spend enough time with real people).

Nader organizations—the U.S. Public Interest Research Group, the Center for Study of Responsive Law, and the Public Citizen's Fund for a Clean Congress—have proposed such an FCA, and the idea was part of banking-reform legislation introduced in 1991 by Democratic congressmen Charles Schumer and Joseph Kennedy II. Also included in the proposed bill was the requirement that four times a year, all federally insured banks, credit unions, and S&Ls would have to include inserts in their mailings informing customers of their right to join a nationwide financial consumers' organization. But this modest proposal failed to attract a Republican cosponsor and was violently opposed by the ever-vigilant banking lobby. As of this writing, the national FCA's time has not yet come.

Every attempt to set up an FCA on a state level has been defeated as well. Proposals have been introduced in Illinois, New York, California, and Texas; all were swiftly shot down. In Illinois, a law that would have given an FCA access to state mailings was proposed by Pat Quinn, a consumer activist who won the office of state treasurer with an FCA as one of his main planks. The idea was supported by 70 to 80 percent margins in advisory referenda held throughout the state in November 1990. But what the public wanted was not what the banking lobby wanted, and the bill died. Nevertheless, Quinn plans to attempt an FCA in Cook County, which has 40 percent of the state's population.

NO RELIEF FOR THE INSURED

Consumers of insurance (that is, all of us) haven't gotten any further than financial consumers (also all of us). One would think that an insurance-advocacy association would have been formed by now; after all, in what other industry have so many paid so much for so little?

Several sizable companies are in what is politely referred to as a "precarious financial state." One big failure could endanger the annuities of millions of consumers. A cottage in-

dustry of investment advisers sells tip sheets on which
weakened insurance companies to avoid, many charging one
hundred dollars a year for the service. An Insurance Consumers' Association could provide that same information to
its members for one tenth the price.

A proposal to create a state insurance board in Illinois was
quickly squelched, thanks in large part to aggressive lobbying
by the major insurance companies headquartered in the state.
In November 1988, a Nader-type group in California called
Voter Revolt sponsored and won an initiative calling for major
reforms in the industry. Proposition 103 mandated rate roll-
backs, discounts for good drivers, public disclosure of industry
operations, and the formation of a nonprofit corporation to
represent consumers in insurance proceedings. But before the
citizens' insurance board could be set up, the California Supreme Court ruled that the state constitution prohibited a
public initiative from establishing a private corporation.

But consumer advocates remain determined. "We're not
going to quit," says Claude Walker, an aide to Illinois treasurer
Pat Quinn. "Democracy broke out first in Eastern Europe;
maybe next it'll be in Illinois."

THE TEN-MINUTE CITIZEN

A different kind of consumer power can be wielded by a single
person acting alone, doing what so many of us do so well:
using a credit card.

If you like the idea of voting with your money, and giving
your business to a user-responsive organization, consider
Working Assets, a twelve-year-old San Francisco company that
runs a money fund, a credit-card company, and a long-
distance telephone service. Working Assets is pure populist,
capitalistic activism.

Many causes have ties with credit cards and get a small

donation from every dollar charged. The Working Assets Visa card program donates a nickel to a group of "hard-hitting advocacy groups" every time a cardholder makes a purchase on the card, no matter how small.

Every year, more than 100,000 cardholders nominate candidates for the donations. After the nominees are screened for effectiveness and quality, thirty-two organizations are selected for the final pool. At the end of the year, cardholders vote on how to allocate that year's donations. Recently, they decided to give 50 percent of the fund to environmental groups, 22 percent to human-rights organizations, and 14 percent each to peace and economic-justice organizations.

Since the program was started in 1986, it has generated nearly two million dollars for more than one hundred organizations, including Greenpeace, Amnesty International, the American Civil Liberties Union, the Environmental Defense Fund, the Children's Defense Fund, the Rainforest Action Network, Oxfam America, and Planned Parenthood.

What's more, every bill includes a message about a current issue. If you agree with the advisory's premise—for example, that the United States should join the international agreement to prohibit the production of chlorofluorocarbons—you check the appropriate box, and Working Assets will send a letter in your name to your congressman.

This "charge card citizenship" gets to the problem of how to generate activism among people who don't have the time to do all those good things they know they should; people whom Working Assets founder Peter Barnes calls ten-minute citizens.

Working Assets' long-distance phone service has an even more innovative feature. Each month, the telephone bill lists two current issues, such as the abortion gag rule or Northwest deforestation. On Free Speech Day, the first Monday of every month, subscribers can call targeted political or corporate leaders for free (they are even given the White House number and urged to call the president) to voice their opinion. Calls to those numbers on other days are given a 10 percent discount. Working Assets will also send well-argued Citizen-Letters for a fraction of Western Union's charge. In April 1992, more than 20 percent of subscribers called Secretary of the Interior Manuel Lujan's office to voice their concern over the Endangered Species Act.

"Democracy is not just about voting," says Peter Barnes. "It's about ongoing dialogue between the people and their representatives. That dialogue has been withering in America. Who better than a phone company to help bring it back to life?" (A print advertisement for Working Assets features a protester making a popular obscene gesture and the headline "Twenty years later, we've given people a better way to put this finger to use.")

· XII ·

Community Power

HOW TO FIGHT BACK

Community survival and good manufacturing jobs are one and the same. Low-paying service jobs and part-time jobs—the kind that the American economy has been producing so abundantly over the last twelve years—won't do it. "Access to manufacturing jobs is the only way up for those kids now on crack," says Jim Benn, executive director of the Federation for Industrial Retention & Renewal.

For a decade, however, communities nationwide have been powerless as manufacturing facilities close because a distant management or a corporate raider decided that a plant wasn't profitable "enough." And when this occurs, the pain, frustration, and anger are as great as if the community had been hit by a natural disaster. If we have hundreds of millions, even billions of dollars to pour into hurricane-hit areas, and to fix man-made muck-ups like the S&L mess and the L.A. riots, why can't we equip communities to respond to the quiet plant-closing catastrophes as well? As it is now, governments and employees can do almost nothing to influence economic decisions that affect hundreds of thousands of lives and livelihoods. Enabling government and citizens' groups to play a role in large plant-closing decisions *before* a crisis occurs should be seen as another form of crime and disaster prevention.

The Federation for Industrial Retention & Renewal, a group of thirty-two affiliated organizations—mostly community-based coalitions of religious, labor, and other groups—is dedicated to this uphill battle of standing up and saying "No," or at least "Wait a minute," to sudden plant closings. Thus far, the FIRR, which is active in twenty-seven cities, has lost most of its battles with industry. But over the past decade they have developed a number of techniques that can help economically viable but threatened businesses to continue operating, even under new ownership.

At the very least, such approaches put some power back into the hands of local communities without hindering the ability of companies to make their own economic decisions and to adjust to changing circumstances.

THE POWER OF EMINENT DOMAIN
One tool is the threat of an eminent-domain seizure to stop the dismantling of a shut-down plant until an alternative use can be devised.

Eminent domain is the power of government to acquire private property for a public good. The railroads were built using eminent domain; so were some of the national parks; and more recently, it has been used for urban renewal, to evict people whose property stands in the way of a new highway or even a shopping center.

One of the earliest invocations of eminent domain for industrial retention was in New Bedford, Massachusetts, in 1984. Gulf + Western had announced the closing of the Morse Tool Cutting plant, and appeals to reconsider made by community groups and the affected union had failed. Finally, the works were sold to a local buyer after city officials threatened to take it over *to prevent the destruction of the common public good of employment.*

More recently, the power of eminent domain was actually wielded for the first time, as the Steel Valley Authority, an industrial-development group active in the mill towns south of Pittsburgh—one of the areas hardest hit by industrial dislocation in America—blocked the destruction of a hundred-year-old bakery that had been shut down in 1989 following corporate restructuring by its parent, Continental-Ralston-Purina. As it turned out, the old plant was indeed worthless, so the SVA and the bakery workers, with the help of a coalition including the mayor and city council of Pittsburgh, the state AFL-CIO, and church leaders, organized a new corporation structured around an employee stock-ownership plan. Financing was provided by two regional investor groups, state pension funds, and a bank consortium, as well as government agencies and several foundations. Local supermarkets kicked in with a $12 million sales order the first year.

The new 102,000 square-foot City Pride Bakery, owned by regional investors, neighborhood groups, and employees, opened in 1992. Of the 250 jobs originally lost, 100 were recreated, and the bakery hopes to have 300 positions altogether within three years.

Community organizers see such efforts as the wave of the future, in which communities can raise plant closing issues to the highest political levels.

"The big message," says the FIRR's Jim Benn, "is 'You can fight back!' "

REZONING
Usually, tracts of land are zoned for residential or commercial use, and manufacturing locates wherever it may in catchall

areas. That is why so many industrial zones are hodgepodges of factories, warehouses, artists' studios, and parking lots. To reverse the trend toward gentrification and deindustrialization, certain areas could be rezoned so that *only* manufacture can take place there, keeping out developers, just as residential areas are protected from auto-body shops and fast-food joints.

Such a zone was established in West Berkeley, California, as part of a total rezoning of the city. The West Berkeley plan also proscribes activities that significantly increase pollution and warns major polluters that they must comply with all environmental laws.

Other community development coalitions are now pushing for this kind of zoning all over the country.

SOCIAL ACCOUNTING

Social-cost analysis—accounting that tries to quantify the total social costs that occur when a plant is closed and jobs are lost—was developed by a Chicago group called the Midwest Center for Labor. It allows communities to estimate as precisely as possible what a plant closing will cost in lost taxes, added expenditures, eliminated jobs, and loss of business to local enterprises.

Such an analysis enables government to make a hard-headed decision on whether to seek alternatives to a plant closing, and to determine how much it should be willing to spend to keep a plant open. Above all, it gives affected individuals a weapon stronger than a cry of pain or an appeal for justice or charity. It endows them with the magic numbers that can show to what extent lives and local economies will be disrupted by shutdowns. It puts the current weapon of choice—the bottom line—at the service of communities.

Jim Benn says, "When you consider in the accounting all the costs to government of dealing with all the human problems, the loss of the tax base, the collapsing real estate markets, the ripple effect on retailers and other businesses in the community, the effects on suppliers and consumers—when you add all that up, then the preservation of a facility operating on even a marginal profit can be worth it."

The FIRR used social-cost analysis during a lengthy recent battle in New York, when Taystee, the last of the city's big bakeries, was shut down without warning by its owner, Stroehmann, a Pennsylvania-based company, in spite of Stroehmann's having been given $780,000 in tax breaks, a discount on utility rates, and triple tax exemption on a $5.2 million bond issue to pay for the Taystee acquisition only three years earlier. (The quick corporate pullout demonstrated the shortcomings of the increasingly discredited strategy of bribing big employers to locate or remain in communities. Aficionados of enterprise zones, which use tax breaks to entice companies into otherwise undesirable areas, should heed the warning.)

Social accounting made it clear just how much the bakery closing would cost the borough of Queens, site of the Taystee plant. Over two years, a total of 1385 workers will probably lose their jobs, including Taystee's 510 unionized, mostly minority staff and an estimated 875 employees of companies supplying goods and services to the bakery, retail stores, and other businesses dependent upon the Taystee payroll—a ripple effect of unemployment. Those workers who find new jobs, the analysis showed, can expect to earn less than two thirds of their former salaries.

The plant closing will cost local, state, and federal governments $32 million in tax revenues and an additional $10 million in additional expenditures on increased unemployment compensation and welfare costs.

As for the human costs, studies confirm that dismissed workers are at substantial risk of contracting stress-related diseases and emotional disorders; and they and their families are susceptible to a Pandora's box of social pathologies including increased spousal violence, child abuse, and drug and alcohol addiction.

Clearly, more than one Pennsylvania company's profit-and-loss statement is at stake here. Social accounting demonstrates that it can be as important for the government to take a stronger lead in its stewardship of the economic order as it is to take responsibility for maintaining law and order.

In the Taystee case, New York's Industrial Development Agency did order Stroehmann to repay its tax waivers, citing the company's violation of its financing agreement with the city. This $780,000 will be used to help laid-off workers open a new employee-owned bakery, to be modeled on Pittsburgh's City Pride.

Angry workers have also mounted a boycott against Taystee, and city officials have debated canceling their commitment to buy $900,000 worth of Taystee bread a year for prisons and shelters. But that won't bring back the jobs, and Stroehmann threatened to lay off an additional six hundred sales and distribution employees if a city boycott occurred. It didn't.

What additional measures would give communities and employees better bargaining power in these kinds of cases? No one disputes the right, often the necessity, of a company to relocate where labor and production costs are cheaper. But is there any way to curb the unilateral corporate power over "disposable factories" and "throwaway people" and at least mitigate the damage?

Here is a partial wish list of community activists:

SIT DOWN AND TALK
Advocates want plant-closing laws improved beyond the current sixty-day required notice. One proposal would force a company to sit down with representatives of local government,

the community, and workers to consider all possible alternatives to a shutdown. This would also give employee groups and other potential purchasers time to put together financing so that a possibly profitable plant could be saved.

EARLY WARNING

Many groups are also trying to establish industrial-planning bodies with wide community participation and a right-to-know policy concerning major employers' production plans, technological investments, and ways of marketing. The purpose: avoiding big unpleasant surprises. A community would presumably gain some forewarning of corporate problems and plans.

The Steel Valley Authority, the South Chicago Jobs Authority, and other advocacy groups already have "early-warning networks" that try to identify companies at risk of shutting down. Time is critical in preparing a successful response to a crisis, because shutdowns and destruction of plant facilities can happen very fast.

RAISE THE EXIT COSTS

Many European countries have statutorily required severance schedules, specifying how much pay dismissed workers are entitled to for every year of employment. In the United States, only Maine and Hawaii have such laws (in Maine, for example, a person is entitled to one week's pay for every working year). Most union contracts already have severance provisions, but the vast majority of American workers aren't represented by unions.

The majority of companies also don't provide any retraining assistance to laid-off workers; right now, the public bears most of those costs. Some large, unionized companies provide such help, including General Motors, which since 1984 has had a program that is jointly managed, paid for, and monitored with the United Auto Workers. Sizable nonunion companies could be mandated to establish such programs with workers' councils, while smaller businesses might be required to pay a head tax per laid-off worker to cover tuition at a local community college.

The point is to do something to stack the corporate balance sheet against plant closings, to prevent companies from heaping the human costs onto employees and the public and to give companies a greater incentive to improve their productivity by pursuing the high-wage, high-skills approach.

CLAW-BACKS AND TIT FOR TAT

A few states have passed laws known as claw-backs, which state that if, in return for a tax abatement or other public subsidy, a company promises to create one hundred jobs, and then creates only fifty, they must pay back half the benefit. Or that if a company relocates within a short time after having received such subsidies, they must cough up whatever they saved in taxes.

Indiana's even stricter regulations require companies to meet annual hurdles (number of jobs created, et cetera) in order to keep their eligibility for tax abatements. Variations on this theme can be found in New Haven, Duluth, and St. Paul.

Under consideration elsewhere in the country is the requirement that companies post a "community bond" in the form of an escrow account, guaranteeing continued revenues for schools, roads, and the like should a company relocate.

As Greg Leroy of Chicago's Midwest Center for Labor Research put it, "We would love to see some of these ideas put in place on a national level, but the enemy has pretty much captured the Capitol." He adds that the important elements of industrial and social policy (unemployment com-

pensation, advance notice of shutdowns, retraining of dislocated workers) became national policy only after trickling up
from the local and state level, and that plant-closing legislation
will be no different.

A CAPITAL FUND

One idea that has not yet seen the light of day anywhere is
an "Industrial Capital Fund," which might take equity positions in enterprises when a social cost/benefit analysis shows
that an intervention is justified, and when independent economic feasibility studies show that the enterprise is in fact
viable. Such a fund could be an offshoot of a new American
Investment Bank and, like the International Finance Corporation of the World Bank, would make direct investments in
promising private companies in less-developed areas within
the United States.

To keep it from turning into a politicized financial boondoggle, any such public investment should be strictly contingent on a preponderance of private capital in the deal. No
one benefits from politically correct but economically foolish
investment.

MAKING IT EXPENSIVE TO MOVE

The ultimate problem facing American workers and America's
manufacturing base is not the factory that shuts down or heads
for greener pastures in the next state, but the company that
flees the country altogether. The globalization of the international economy, in which jobs are becoming as mobile as
capital, is the most important economic transformation of the
past two decades. It amounts to a shift in power from the
hands of democratic government and its average citizens to

the holders of private capital and private corporations, and we've just begun to see the implications.

The trend makes it harder for governments to establish environmental, labor, health, and safety regulations; for increasingly, if a major company doesn't like these rules, it can leave. Among those it leaves behind are the country's average wage earners. Many economists predict that the decline in American wages will continue for another twenty to twenty-five years, until worldwide labor costs reach some kind of rough equilibrium. This is grim news indeed if your job can be performed by a smart, eager young person who is willing to play the slave for one seventh of your salary. (Free-market economists aren't generally in that vulnerable position, which may help explain why they view the emerging global marketplace with relative equanimity.)

Call it global optimization, or manufacturing miscegenation, or whatever you want, it is hard to find a mass-produced product in the United States today that doesn't have an international parentage. U.S. companies employ about 2 million workers in low-wage countries abroad, many of them producing goods for the American market. It is impossible to determine the net number of U.S. jobs that have been lost due to offshore production. Significantly, considering the reams of statistics that pour out of government agencies, these employment figures have not been gathered in any systematic way.

But certainly, the vast majority of the more than 500,000 ill-paid Mexicans employed by American companies are displacing American workers. Over the past five years, U.S. companies have invested $11.6 billion in Mexican plants. More than 100,000 Mexicans now work for U.S. auto companies alone, for wages of two dollars an hour and less.

By many economists' reckoning, more American jobs have been created than lost as trade with Mexico has grown, and Mexicans buy more U.S. trucks and computers. According to

Gary Hufbauer of the Institute for International Economics, the net job gain has been 175,000 since 1989.

The trend has also helped many consumers, who sometimes—but not always—get cheaper products. But again, no one in government has bothered to calculate how much the average American will have to pay for the additional welfare, unemployment compensation, law enforcement, criminal justice, and private security systems born of the disruption of the livelihoods of so many citizens. These largely public costs, dumped on taxpayers by fleeing companies, might well outweigh any private gains we may realize from our cheaper toasters and blue jeans. "The trouble with our trade policy," says Pat Choate, a political economist and author of *Agents of Influence*, "is that we want cheap goods for our consumers, while other nations want their consumers to be rich enough to afford any goods that they want."

When the proposed Free Trade Agreement with Mexico goes into effect, protecting the rights of foreign investors, American companies will be even more willing to risk greater investment in Mexico, with its irresistible labor force of almost 30 million people desperate to work for wages that average one seventh to one fourteenth of ours. The admittedly rough estimates of the effects of the Free Trade Agreement conclude that after several years, a few thousand American jobs will be created as Mexicans buy more products made in the United States; in the meanwhile, more than *100,000* American jobs will have been lost.

The trouble is, the people losing their jobs don't necessarily have the advanced skills to fill the new slots being created. Nor will the Mexicans be able to buy the American goods that create employment here unless they make considerably more money than they are being paid today. Mexican wages have actually lagged behind the rising cost of living in the past decade. In 1981, the average salary of a worker in the *ma-*

quiladora industry along the border was $1.12 an hour. By the end of 1989, the wage, adjusted for inflation, had fallen to $0.56 an hour. A cursory tour of the fetid slums of the border towns, fouled by chemical pollutants, and of the factories, where adolescents work a full day for that exploitative wage, will disabuse anyone of the notion that Mexican *maquiladora* workers are benefiting at the expense of Americans. At the moment, both countries' "blue collars" are losing.

Ironically, those who tout free trade with Mexico have by and large been silent on the issue of Mexican labor abuse. Yet if such oppression ended, the free traders' rosy predictions of common benefits might really come true.

In the United States, the pain and sense of betrayal that is felt by the hundreds of thousands—if not millions—of dislocated workers and their families is spreading like a malignancy on the body politic. And no democracy can afford not to address it.

Some observers, including author William Greider, believe that globalized production is "the largest challenge confronting American democracy."

Free trade isn't the problem, nor is the free movement of capital, which we could scarcely do anything about even if we tried. The problem and the solution is to make American companies accept their obligations to their own country. They need to display a little patriotism in return for the security of being chartered American corporations protected by the political stability, the respect for contracts, and the military muscle that distinguish the United States from so much of the rest of the world.

There are ample resources in American corporate law to enforce the notion of the corporation as a collective citizen, with responsibilities as well as rights. Legal scholar James Boyd White (quoted in *The Good Society*, a thoughtful book about American democracy and our social ills) says:

To say that a corporation's only goal is to make money would be to define the business corporation—for the first time in American or English law as I understand it—as a kind of shark that lives off the community rather than as an important agency in the construction, maintenance, and transformation of our shared lives.

It is reasonable to require, for example, that if companies like General Motors and Ford and Proctor-Silex and Levi Strauss wish to continue as American, rather than Mexican or Taiwanese, companies, they should make some kind of contribution to the American people and communities they are abandoning, like a shiftless parent who runs out on an irritating baby and never comes back.

Here are some of the ways we could make American multinationals more accountable:

- Currently, there are no distinctions between layoffs due to falling sales and company losses, and layoffs due to corporate restructurings and relocations abroad. Whatever the cause, American workers today can be discarded like used Kleenex. All too typical was one sixty-one-year-old woman in Paterson, New Jersey, who worked for thirty-three years for a manufacturer before being laid off because her company was opening a new plant in Mexico. She was given one month's health coverage and three thousand dollars in severance pay.

Several proposed pieces of legislation introduced in 1992 would require employers that close down a production facility in the United States while increasing production in a low-wage country to provide four to six months' advance notice to employees (currently the requirement is sixty days). They would pay dismissed workers from one to four weeks' severance pay for each year of employment, one year of continued health benefits, and reimbursement for retraining and relocation expenses up to ten thousand dollars.

These requirements would begin to put the United States in line with other industrialized (one is tempted to say civilized) countries. In Italy, for example, firms shutting down facilities are typically required to pay workers *one month's* salary per year of employment.

• Incredibly, U.S. taxpayers currently *subsidize* corporations to export jobs. Companies get to deduct from their federal income taxes expenses associated with closing down domestic plants. Those moving production out of the country should kiss that little goodie bye-bye.

• Senator Howard Metzenbaum's Save American Jobs bill would also make it harder for companies that export jobs to receive government contracts. In 1990, the federal government gave out $171 billion in federal contracts, including $4.2 billion to General Motors, which is eliminating 74,000 jobs in this country and expanding its operations in Mexico, where it is already the largest private employer. The proposed legislation gives companies that have not relocated operations abroad a preference in the awarding of government contracts.

Again, this is standard operating procedure in Europe. A recent report by the Office of Technology Assessment found that many EEC leaders encourage "inward investment in firms that promise to create well-paid knowledge-intensive jobs and to transfer valuable technology to local supply firms." These policies are encouraged by a combination of strict rules of origin and *discriminatory public-procurement policies*, and are "pushing foreign firms to manufacture in Europe rather than to export to Europe."

If this is what our competitors are doing, why on

earth are we pushing our industries *out* of the country?

▪ Federal taxpayers underwrite billions of dollars in government grants, loans, and loan guarantees to American companies every year. In 1990 and 1991, General Electric received more than $1.6 million in federal R&D grants and Export-Import Bank loans and guarantees. That was after G.E. had moved thousands of electrical-industry jobs out of the country.

The Metzenbaum bill would prohibit employers who relocate operations abroad from receiving federal grants and loans for a period of five years.

▪ The United States and other industrialized countries set standards for international banks; there is no reason why there couldn't be similar international agreements setting minimum standards for health and safety, wages, and labor law, as well as the means of enforcing them. Lane Kirkland, president of the AFL-CIO, has suggested, for example, that the denial of workers' rights be legally defined as an unfair trading practice.

If any country violated the standards, we would simply outlaw importation of its offending products. The United States prohibits the importation of products made by coerced prison labor and goods made from the bodies of endangered species. Why don't we also prohibit goods made by child labor, or made under conditions violating our own health, safety, and environmental standards?

Finally, American workers should not have to compete with foreign workers whose wages are kept down not by "an iron law of economics but by an iron hand of oppression," as Jeff Faux of the Economic Policy Institute expressed it in testimony on the Metzenbaum bill. American workers should not be penalized for living in a country where basic human rights, environmental safeguards, and collective bargaining are respected—if they continue to be, those rights and safeguards themselves will be endangered.

• If Mexico, our new partner in free trade, can't afford to enforce an environmental cleanup, then the United States needs to consider an assistance program, similar to the financial help that the EEC provides its new, poorer members. The money could come from a tax on U.S. corporations that operate plants in Mexico or from the revenues from the remaining tariffs on Mexican goods. The recent news that several dozen babies on both sides of the U.S.-Mexican border were born without brains, possibly because of pollution associated with local *maquiladora* operations, might help prompt action.

WHAT YOU CAN DO

Citizens could try a little persuasion of their own, by boycotting products made abroad under questionable conditions. A list of the "Plant Closing Dirty Dozen" is now put out by the Federation of Industrial Retention & Renewal, exposing the "corporations that have exhibited the most irresponsible behavior." The offenders making consumer products abroad included Hanson PLC/Smith Corona, Grand Metropolitan/ Green Giant, American Mills/United Foods, and Farah Manufacturing.

Not all of those on the 1992 list had shifted jobs out of the country. One company, Vanalco Aluminum Company of Seattle, earned its place by using more than $700,000 of federal job-training monies to "train" workers in jobs they already had, and then overstating wages to inflate reimbursements.

Also on the FIRR list was American Home Products' subsidiary Wyeth-Averst in Great Valley, Pennsylvania, which reduced the jobs in its suburban Philadelphia pharmaceutical plant from 700 in 1989 to approximately 125 by early 1992. Nearly all the job loss was due to movement of production to a tax-sheltered plant in Puerto Rico, despite a 1987 Puerto Rican law that explicitly prohibits the use of the tax subsidy if a transfer of jobs from the mainland United States is involved.

One company that packed off to a *maquiladora* was Cleveland-based NACCO Industries, which acquired the unprofitable Hamilton Beach in 1990 and merged it with its Proctor-Silex division. In the spring of 1991, NACCO announced a restructuring and transferred eight hundred jobs in a Proctor-Silex plant in Southern Pines, North Carolina, to a facility in Juarez, Mexico. The American workers had been making $7.50 an hour. They were offered no severance pay, no health insurance extensions, and no retraining assistance.

The workers subsequently documented over forty cases of cancer among plant employees, and it was revealed that barrels of toxic waste were buried beneath the facility. Sitting on NACCO's board all through the controversy were Environmental Defense Fund trustee Frank E. Taplin and Nature Conservancy president and CEO John C. Sawhill.

Another direct-action campaign is being mounted by more than sixty environmental, religious, community and labor organizations that have united to pressure U.S. transnational corporations to adopt more socially responsible practices toward Mexican laborers.

The Coalition for Justice in the Maquiladoras has drawn up guidelines on environmental contamination, violations of workers' rights, and workplace safety. Corporate compliance with the standards will be monitored, and the information will be provided to public and private investors and brought up at shareholder meetings. The group will also pressure Congress to incorporate its standards of conduct into any trade agreement with the Mexican government.

If it can win enough support, on campuses, within con-gregations, and wherever else concerned citizens gather these days, the CJM could gain as much strength as the anti-apartheid disinvestment movement did in the seventies and eighties, with even more effect on the standard of living and the economic well-being of all Americans.

If capital has no borders, and jobs have no borders, then neither do corporate responsibility and ethical behavior.

· XIII ·

You Can Take Your Pension with You

If you didn't get rich in the 1980s and you don't work for the government and you're a young blue-collar man or a single woman under fifty, how secure a senior citizen will you be in the twenty-first century? About as secure as people were in the 1930s, when old-age insurance was invented.

Two thirds of Americans have no savings other than the equity in their homes and their pensions. And here's what your private retirement pension looks like, after the 1980s got through with it:

- More than half of all workers have no private pension plan at all, largely because they aren't offered them. Only about 40 percent of all workers participate in company pension plans, down from 49 percent in 1979.
- Fewer than 30 percent of workers in private industry are covered by a defined-benefit plan—one that guar-

antees a fixed retirement check every month. And their number is declining as well.

- Because the great majority of private pension plans require ten years of employment before a worker is eligible to collect, half the workers who are covered by a plan are not yet vested. If they move on to another job, they get no pension at all.

- Corporations removed $21 billion from their employees' pension plans during the 1980s, often using the money to pay for the gigantic debt incurred during the decade's borrowing binge. Outright looting stripped the pension assets of people who worked for Robert Maxwell and his ilk, and pervasive misappropriation of funds and terminations of plans left millions of other employees with reduced or uninsured benefits.

A tear in the private safety net has turned into a gaping hole.

Workers in the private sector now receive far smaller pensions than the 17 percent of workers who are employed by local, state, or federal governments (whose pensions are also usually indexed for inflation). And for women, private pensions are especially, ludicrously small: Single women receive a median payment of $2,153 a year, compared with $3,820 a year for men—not enough in either case. From 1976 to 1988, the amount of single women's pensions fell from about three fourths of single men's to about half. Married women get even less compared to married men. When it comes to retirement, women still can't eat without being invited to a man's table.

It has been forecast that *40 percent of single baby-boom women will live in poverty in their old age*. So much for feminist progress.

■   ■   ■

There are many reasons for the rapid decline of the private security system: the decline of labor unions and the shrinking of the typical paycheck being the most prominent. Stronger labor laws enabling unions to increase their membership, which is practically synonymous with pension coverage, and a serious increase in the minimum wage, enabling lower-wage workers to save more, would do much to repair the fraying private safety net. If we can't strengthen the inadequate private pension system, we're either going to see a nasty resurgence of poverty among older people—a new age of "throwaway grannies"—or we're going to have to nationalize our entire retirement system, a predictable outcome of the failure of the private sector.

What else can be done?

IT'S OUR MONEY

We could protect the funds set aside for workers' retirement from greedy corporate management by giving employees equal representation on the boards of all single-employer defined-benefit pension plans. This kind of cotrusteeship has worked well in many multiemployer plans. And no one denies that the funds are, after all, not the company's but the employees' money, in the form of deferred compensation.

At the least, joint trusteeship would probably halt one of the favorite corporate tricks of the 1980s, the termination of defined-benefit plans on the grounds that more than sufficient assets had been raised to meet obligations. Never mind that only a few years later, many "overfunded" plans have ended up underfunded, and may eventually have to be bailed out by taxpayers. And never mind that many of the companies that did terminate pension plans then bought uninsured annuities paying smaller benefits and spent the leftover cash on executive perks and servicing corporate debt.

None of that carried any weight when pension power sharing was introduced in 1989 legislation by Democratic congressman Peter J. Visclosky of Indiana. Visclosky's bill was approved in committee only to be shot down on the House floor faster than a one-winged duck. Corporations threatened a mass termination of benefit plans if they were forced to allow workers as cotrustees of their own retirement funds.

YOU CAN TAKE IT WITH YOU

What Americans really need is a portable pension that is tied to the worker and not to the job, an idea that fits the late-twentieth-century reality of multiple jobs and an ever-changing workplace, and which would allow employees to change jobs, or leave and reenter the work force, while their pension rights continued to accrue.

Some pension plans, for transportation and construction workers and university professors, for instance, are already portable within an industry. But when most workers shift between two employers with retirement plans, they lose a significant part of their pensions. What is called for is a mechanism to move our pensions between incompatible plans to guarantee that we don't lose our retirement security when we quit to take care of children or older parents, when our company lays off 10 percent of its employees and we find ourselves "redundant," or when we want to move on and be more productive somewhere else.

Under a "Portable Pension Plan" every worker would have an account in a fund administered by a government agency, and both worker and employer would make matching tax-exempt contributions. If a worker changed jobs, the funds accumulated would transfer into the new employer's pension plan or be left in the central fund. If a person became self-employed or unemployed, he or she could continue making tax-deductible contributions to the PPP up to a set limit.

The idea would increase savings. It would build financial

security for millions of people whose lives don't allow for lock-step employment over decades: that is, most women and an increasing number of men. It would allow Social Security to revert to its original role as a supplement to retirement income. It would facilitate greater worker mobility and, probably, productivity. It would cut down on some of the worst unproductive excesses of finance capitalism, because you can be damn sure that people wouldn't choose to sink their retirement savings into some of the black holes corporations poured it into during the merger mania of the 1980s.

Women's organizations might breathe life into the Portable Pension idea through research and lobbying efforts, for the entire retirement and pension system, as it stands, is incredibly skewed against women.

Maybe it's not an accident, then, that the most radical pension-reform idea I've encountered comes from a female economics professor at the University of Notre Dame. Theresa Ghilarducci suggests that we simply scrap the entire existing system—gradually phasing out the 500,000 private employee-pension plans—and replace it with a universal advance-capitalized national fund (or several regional funds), which would have portable credits and benefits a worker would retain throughout his or her life. Tax exemptions for employer-sponsored pension contributions would gradually be replaced by a new taxing mechanism to support government contributions to each worker's account.

Such a fund would eliminate the burden of employer contributions, which currently amount to one third of labor costs—a cost not borne by companies anywhere else in the world. It would also pay out benefits far more equitably than our present retirement system, which does nothing for the 47 million working Americans who have no private-pension coverage at all.

· XIV ·

What to Do about Welfare

All the attention paid to welfare masks the deplorable societal neglect of the many poor people who get out of bed every morning, go to work, obey the law, worry about street crime, and pay their taxes. The twenty to thirty million working poor—who used to be called "the deserving poor," as opposed to the shiftless other kind—are the least-assisted group in the economy by far; they also pay the highest marginal tax rate.

Thanks to a serious flaw in the tax code, people earning between $13,000 and $20,000 have to give up forty-one cents in income taxes and government benefits for every dollar they earn over $13,000. When state taxes and the loss of welfare benefits (including Medicaid) and food stamps are figured in, some of the working poor are actually worse off by working more. Their marginal tax rate effectively exceeds 100 percent—meaning that the government takes away more than they earn over a certain amount.

All this has to be kept in mind when we lecture the poor

to "work harder." Since they are unable to take congressional staffers to lunch or provide lawmakers with plush speaking engagements, plane trips, and slush funds, they are the invisible members of our political economy.

A STAKE IN THE SYSTEM

If we want to improve productivity and the work ethic, the answer would be to give low-income people greater incentives to save and accumulate capital, to give them a hand in building a stake in the economy before they need a handout that mires them in dependency. This is what Margaret Thatcher had in mind when she sold British public-housing units to their tenants.

Today, the bottom 90 percent of the American population controls about the same amount of assets as the top 1 percent—not the kind of distribution that breeds enterprise or loyalty to the system.

One remedy would be to create special Individual Development Accounts (IDAs), tax-exempt savings accounts that could be used only for asset-building purposes, that is, financing a postsecondary education, buying a home, starting a business, or accumulating a retirement fund.

The present system already encourages some asset building through the federal home-mortgage tax deduction and by making contributions to private pensions tax exempt. These two privileges have created the bulk of the country's household-asset accumulation. But these programs haven't done much for the working poor. Many if not most have been priced out of the housing market and have no private pensions.

An IDA for pensions could be developed by expanding SEPs (Simplified Employee Pensions), which allow workers to contribute directly to a plan if their employers cannot, or if they are self-employed. The government could opt to match the individual's contribution, giving the low-income worker a subsidy similar to that received through the tax system by the more affluent. IDAs would operate like any defined-contribution retirement plan, with the money going into bank savings, a money-market fund, stocks, or bonds.

The IDA system might also improve our low-income housing policy, which now revolves primarily around rent subsidies and giving private developers incentives to build low-income housing. Why not bypass developers, landlords, and bureaucrats and channel the money directly to the public by matching individual contributions to tax-free IDAs for home down payments? Research shows that once poor families have been able to scrape together a down payment, they keep up with their mortgages as well as anybody else.

If an IDA program were targeted strictly at the working poor, the costs could range from less than $1 billion a year for a modest program to $15 billion for a comprehensive system of matching grants for education, housing, self-employment, and retirement (IDAs for education would not be necessary if other ideas for providing universal higher education were implemented).

In all cases the government could match, by whatever ratio chosen, the contribution made by the individual as a form of investment in that person's future.

The IDA idea has all the elements of the "new paradigm" of the 1990s' socioeconomic policy: It moves away from government handouts and bureaucracies to a societal backing of people who are trying to better themselves.

SACRED BULLS

One of my favorite solutions to the problems facing hard-working, single, poor mothers—and single middle-class mothers, for that matter—is simple: Find the fathers of their children and make them pay up. It takes two to make a baby, and where are the fathers of all of those children on welfare? It is highly unlikely that any of those babies were immaculately conceived. Let's forget about sacred cows for a moment, and turn our attention to the sacred bulls.

It has been calculated that if every absentee father paid the income-based child-support mandated in Wisconsin, the poverty rate among single-parent children in the United States would drop by 48 percent.

But of course, they don't pay. The lawlessness around this issue is staggering: Eighty percent of all welfare-supported children have an absent father who earns, on average, $15,000 a year. But only 15 percent of those children receive child-support payments.

Through 1989, a total of $23 billion in child-support payments had been court ordered. Of that amount, only $5.8 billion, about 25 percent, had been paid. The states manage to collect about $1.25 billion of delinquent payments, but unpaid child support grows by $3 billion a year. Roughly, only half of the five million women with legal orders for child support receive the full amount. Twenty-five percent get no money at all.

The men involved, by the way, are from all income levels, all races, all religions. Nonsupport of children is an equal-opportunity crime, perpetrated by men who leave overburdened women (and the rest of us) to pick up the bills. It is hard not to read in this scenario a massive indifference to, if not contempt for, the responsibilities of raising children and for children themselves.

The solution is breathtakingly obvious, and would no doubt be in effect already if there were more women in Congress. The federal government has to take over the responsibility for enforcing child support from states and counties, whose jurisdiction and resources are entirely too limited for the broad scope of the problem. All states should do what many are already doing: require that both parents' Social Security numbers be recorded on every birth certificate. Noncustodial parents, easily traced, would have their child-support payments deducted from their paychecks, and the money would be mailed directly to the parent who is taking care of the child.

A plan to accomplish this by transferring responsibility for child-support collection from states to the IRS has been proposed by a liberal/conservative House coalition led by Democrat Thomas J. Downey of New York and Republican Henry Hyde of Illinois.

To work, a federal child-support effort would have to have the enforcement powers of the IRS, including the power to seize assets. Deadbeat parents should also be reported to credit agencies, so that they couldn't borrow money for themselves while neglecting their children.

Dennis Bannon, the head of a private collection agency now involved in child-support cases, thinks that an all-out effort could probably recover $11 billion to $12 billion of unpaid child support. He and many others would like to see all national licensing—for doctors, lawyers, pilots, et cetera—linked to compliance, so that nonsupport would be grounds for losing one's professional credentials.

And why not award a bounty to anyone turning in a child dodger?

The question is why we don't do any of this. Consider what is at stake: the well-being of millions of children in poverty; the expenditure of billions of tax dollars for child welfare; a massive evasion of the law; and a thumb-your-nose attitude toward "family values," which in the United States are certainly honored more in the breach than in the observance.

Tough talk is useless; we need tough laws against what

Dennis Bannon calls "the worst crime a person can commit —neglecting his kids."

■ ■ ■

In the absence of national wage withholding, backlogged state enforcement agencies are pretty much incapable of tracking down many vanished fathers, especially those who have moved to other states. For women with the means to do so, a better recourse is to go to one of the new private, for-profit child-support collection agencies. Such agencies are now operating in at least twenty-one states, mostly in the Northeast (New Jersey and New York have two of the worst rates of child-support compliance in the country). The agencies generally charge an application fee of twenty-five to thirty-five dollars and keep about 25 percent of what they collect from the absent parent. Legal expenses may be taken on top of that. The firms don't accept clients on welfare because whatever they were able to collect from the nonsupportive parent would have to go to the state as compensation for welfare payments.

It is sad to say that private detective-type agencies represent the best hope of recovering the billions of dollars that are legally owed to millions of American children. Perhaps that befits a crime-fascinated culture, but is it civilized or becoming to a "great power"?

MICROLENDING

People without jobs or hope riot in Los Angeles, and the federal government promises $600 million in disaster relief. Instead of investing a little in people before they grow angry and desperate, we rush in with carloads of money to fix things after they are broken. You do have to wonder about how the federal government defines a "disaster." Obviously, South

Central L.A., not to mention L.A. law enforcement, was a disaster long before the Rodney King decision.

What is needed in L.A. is the same thing that is needed in Mexico City and Manila: economic development. For several years, nonprofit economic-development groups have touted a cost-effective approach called "microlending": that is, lending small amounts of money to disadvantaged people who want to set themselves up in business.

The model for these efforts is the Grameen Bank in Bangladesh, which makes small loans to poor villagers, mostly women. The key to the program's success is that borrowers are organized into small groups that are collectively responsible for repayment of the loans. For a relatively modest amount of capital, Grameen's efforts are credited with raising living standards significantly among its borrowers.

Here is a good example of how we could take decades of economic-development experience abroad and apply the lessons here at home, in our own underdeveloped areas. In poor American communities, there are plenty of potential "microentrepreneurs" who would like to open repair shops, beauty shops, day-care centers, cleaning and tailoring services, modest manufacturing firms, and all the other small businesses that every neighborhood needs.

The federal government actually spends more money assisting individual entrepreneurs overseas than it does in the United States. But in the last few years, some two hundred private nonprofit groups have spread the microenterprise lending idea around *this* country.

Chicago's Women's Self-Employment Project, founded in 1986, is modeled directly on the Grameen Bank. Poor prospective borrowers are helped to organize themselves into small groups, called circles, which undergo six weeks of orientation and subsequently act as their own loan committees. Each circle selects its first members who will receive funds from the project. Each woman chosen can obtain an initial one-year loan of up to fifteen hundred dollars for equipment, inventory, supplies, or marketing.

The interest rate is 15 percent, and repayment begins almost immediately. Only after the first two borrowers in a circle have established a repayment record do the others become eligible for a loan. If anyone in the circle defaults, the others lose their access to funds.

Instead of collateral, peer pressure and group support enforce discipline. And it works: As of 1991, not one borrower among seventeen groups of borrowers from the $190,000 fund had defaulted. One early borrower started a dress shop that buys from other women in the program; another launched a temp agency for seamstresses; a third has a small baby-food business.

Similar peer-group lending programs have been launched in Arkansas by the Southern Development Bankcorporation; in North Carolina; in St. Paul, Minnesota (Women Venture); and in Native American communities, including the Lakota Fund in South Dakota.

In some ways, these funds resemble the family lending groups that have helped immigrant South Koreans become such successful small entrepreneurs. In those groups, members contribute to a pool of capital and lend all the money to one person for a year. As the funds are repaid, the next loan is made, and so on until the last family member receives a loan. The group's cohesion and the sense of shame attached to failure are critical to the idea's success.

None of the proponents of microlending believe that it is a panacea. It is hard enough for the most dedicated, advantaged person in the world to make a go of a small business, much less a former welfare recipient. By one estimate, only 1 to 10 percent of those who may be judged suitable for self-employment can actually make it work, be they dislocated workers or homemakers looking for flexible work or immigrants with language problems or someone trying to live clean or to get off welfare.

Microloan funds are also not generally profitable, because of the need to offer training and counseling to prospective borrowers.

Still, microlending is an important idea because it offers an opportunity for people to help themselves. As one lender puts it, "Economic development is what people *do*, not what we can do *for* them. It's getting people economically active; it's not income maintenance."

In contrast, the hated welfare system discourages people from making any effort to better themselves.

For example, AFDC, the basic welfare program, does not allow any recipient to have more than one thousand dollars in personal assets. There is no distinction between personal and business property, so a person owning a sewing machine or rug-cleaning equipment might become ineligible for all assistance, including Medicaid. Similarly, if a welfare recipient has a car worth more than fifteen hundred dollars, he becomes ineligible. (Does that sound paternalistic?) That rules out any vehicle needed for business activities.

Many municipalities also have limits or outright prohibitions on home-based businesses. Fear of sweatshops may be legitimate, but local governments have to find a better way to monitor conditions in the workplace than by enforcing bans that stifle home-based business development.

Partly because of pressure from microlending advocates, efforts are under way in Congress to modify some ADFC rules and to put a few million dollars of federal money into microenterprise. The best way to encourage such lending, however, may be to promote the creation of more community development banks and self-help credit unions, and to establish a secondary mortgage agency to purchase their loans (as outlined in Chapter 8, on public-purpose banking).

A FAMILY WAGE

Asked at a town meeting in New Hampshire during his 1992 presidential bid what he would do about welfare, Jerry Brown snapped, "Pay a decent wage."

Asked what he would do about education, the former governor of California said the same thing. "School achievement is very closely correlated with a stable family," he explained. "Nothing is more important for education than a decent family wage."

Sadly, with the average worker's bargaining power now reduced to a smile and a begging bowl, a living wage is getting harder and harder to earn. A 1992 study by the Economic Policy Institute found that wages for the typical American worker had dropped 7.3 percent from 1979 to 1991 (adjusting for inflation). Reductions in pay were greatest for those at the lower end of the scale, but even college-educated men without advanced degrees found their incomes slipping after 1987.

Another study, by the Census Bureau, reported that the proportion of full-time year-round workers getting what it classified as low wages had jumped from 12.1 percent in 1979 to 18 percent in 1990.

The reasons for the deterioration are many: declining union power, the ease with which American companies can shift manufacturing jobs out of the country, and a weaker minimum wage. Let's take a look at what's happened to the floor on wages.

THE BOTTOM DOLLAR

The real value of the minimum wage fell by roughly one third during the 1980s. It was raised in 1989 to the rich sum of

$4.25 an hour, $170 for a forty-hour week. That is still less in real terms than ten years ago, which helps explain why some eleven million Americans in families with at least one working member live in poverty.

How can a public whose income is declining be good for all the other Americans whose job it is to sell things to those same people?

The failure of wages to keep up with the cost of living explains more about the "welfare problem" than most other attempts. The majority of people working at $4.25 an hour are women, many of them supporting children. Minimum wage is not enough to pull their families out of poverty. To make ends meet, many women cycle in and out of the welfare system or try to combine welfare with some kind of ill-paid work.

Contrary to tenacious myth, most welfare mothers don't like the system any better than the rest of us do. (One recipient commented, "Welfare is the worst husband you can have.")

What poor single mothers need is a new husband: a decent wage. What ever happened to the old idea of a family wage, enough to support, say, two children? Shouldn't private industry have to pay, at the very least, a minimum wage that keeps up with inflation?

One response has been that raising the minimum wage would result in fewer jobs, and at some level that has to be true. But the minimum wage in America has fallen so low that the link may not be so strong after all. In fact, a number of recent studies have found no "statistically significant" negative effects on employment from the increases in the minimum wage that took place since the late 1970s.

Most minimum-wage workers labor in private households, on farms, in the food-service industries, and in retail and personal sales. These are the gritty service jobs that can't be packed up and shipped off to Mexico or the Far East. Someone will always have to clean the bathrooms, work in restaurants, pick fruit, and sell clothing, toiletries, and hardware to the middle class. We just might have to pay more for these services, as we have learned to pay more for teachers now that we no longer have a captive pool of female labor.

A modernized minimum wage could exclude certain part-time jobs and jobs in fast-food restaurants, which are often held by teenagers; it could allow for regional differences in labor markets; it could make some distinction between jobs that might be shifted abroad and jobs that are tied to daily American life but easily open to exploitation.

How much would this cost the average taxpayer? It depends on how high an increase we enact. (Bear in mind that only about 5 percent of all workers earn the minimum wage or less.) Higher labor costs are usually passed along in higher prices, and the average family could be forced to spend hundreds of dollars more a year; some businesses, not able to pass along their costs, might forgo expansion or even fold. Other businesses, of course, would blossom on the new purchasing power created by higher wages.

Raising the minimum wage to the levels of the early 1980s, in real terms, and then indexing it to the cost of living would be the least we could do to relieve the poverty of the working poor. We would be paying people for a day's *work*—which is exactly what we say we want. It would be interesting to see what would happen if some brave politician tried to explain all this to the public and asked them to put their money where their mouth is.

EITC: AN ACRONYM ONLY AN ECONOMIST COULD LOVE

Some economists maintain that instead of increasing the minimum wage, it would be better to expand the Earned Income Tax Credit, a cash bonus paid by the federal government to low-wage workers. Currently, working families with incomes of less than $21,250 qualify for income-tax and health-insurance credits of up to $2000. If those credits were expanded by another $1.25 billion a year, as is suggested in Jay Rockefeller's proposed Family Income Security Act, we would end poverty for nearly four million poor Americans, including one of every five poor children, and help another seven million people in families with part-time workers. (Advocates of the $1.25 billion subsidy increase point out that it could be fully financed, with money to spare, if Congress eliminated one of private industry's cushiest subsidies, and charged shipping companies for the full cost of the commercial services provided to them by the Army Corps of Engineers and the Coast Guard.)

The trouble with the EITC, aside from its name, is this: It is a government handout financed by ordinary taxpayers to subsidize employers who pay less than a living wage. Wouldn't it be better to require the market (that is, employers) to pay a decent wage in the first place? Then the market, not the federal government, would decide how much the public would have to pay.

· XV ·

Growth and Equity:
Two Sides of the
Same Coin

A DIET FOR FAT CATS

One of the hottest economic issues during the 1992 electoral season was executive pay, which quickly came to symbolize all the "Me First" excesses and "Après moi le déluge" attitudes of so many business and political "leaders" in the 1980s. The multimillion-dollar pay packages of American executives are to the ailing American economy what Imelda Marcos's three thousand pairs of shoes were to the impoverished Philippines—a powerful statement about insensitivity and glaring inequalities in the system.

The issue caught fire when President Bush took a dozen corporate chief executives with him to Japan, and someone at *The Wall Street Journal* noted that the average annual compensation of those worthies was over $2 million. By comparison, the typical Japanese CEO of a major company makes about $525,000. When asked why the Japanese were willing to work for so much less, executive compensation expert Graef S. Crystal suggested, "Their greed glands are smaller."

There is something rapacious about a few middle-aged men earning salaries of $15 million, $20 million, and, in one case, $78 million a year, particularly when some of these men were presiding over troubled corporations and laying off scores of their employees.

In 1991, for example, when corporate profits fell an estimated 21 percent and worker layoffs were averaging 2600 a day by early November, the average cash payment to chief executives soared to $1.3 million. Counting the value of his stock and stock options, the average CEO made nearly $4 million in 1991. CEOs of major American companies now pay themselves roughly *160 times* the average American wage, a gap that is utterly out of sync in a country that calls itself the "land of opportunity." Opportunity for whom? And for what?

In Japan, the average top executive earns about twenty times more than the average worker; in Germany, it's twenty-one to one. In the United States, the income gap has doubled in the last fifteen years.

Consider the spectacle of William A. Anders, chairman of the General Dynamics Corporation, who in 1991 took home $9.35 million as his part of a top-level pay package that saw twenty-three of the big defense contractor's top executives receive more than $35 million in pay, bonuses, stock, and stock options.

General Dynamics' profits were $331 million that year; meanwhile, the company closed down production lines and fired nearly ten thousand employees from Long Island to Ohio.

The so-called Prince of Pay was Steven J. Ross, who, as head of Warner Communications, Inc., took home about $275 million between 1973 and 1989, just before his company digested Time Inc. in a messy and heavily leveraged takeover meal. In 1990, Ross made $78.2 million (most of it payment for his interest in Warner), while sending out pink slips to hundreds of Time Inc. editors and reporters.

The jolliest greed giants of them all were the auto executives, who paid themselves bonuses in 1991, one of the worst years on record, and told their workers to eat cake. Despite heavy losses and layoffs at his company, Chrysler CEO Lee Iacocca pulled down $4.65 million in direct compensation in 1991, plus 62,500 shares of stock per quarter, worth roughly $5 million by mid-1992. As if that weren't enough to induce a work ethic, Chrysler bought two homes off Mr. Iacocca when he couldn't sell them for the prices he wanted.

A few commentators deplored the heavy attention paid to these various payoffs on the grounds that outrageous as they are, they are as nothing compared to more serious economic issues like productivity and the deficit. But that is missing the point entirely. When high executives pay themselves fortunes that bear little relationship to how their companies are doing and that are completely disconnected from the wages or job security of their employees, they are sending a strong message to the organization. It can be more or less summarized as "Up yours."

That message's negative effect on worker morale, commitment to the job, loyalty to the company, and plain old work ethic cannot be overstated. Anyone who doubts that financial shenanigans in the executive suite have a detrimental effect on productivity is out to an expense-account lunch.

Even compensation schemes linked to actual corporate profits can have a negative effect on productivity, because they undermine long-term capital investments and investments in intangibles like worker training, whose contribution to earnings is not easily measurable. The lush rewards executives arrange for themselves are thus directly related to the failure of American companies to invest in the modernization and innovation they need to compete with their Japanese and German counterparts.

Executive pay packages are therefore a legitimate public concern, particularly because the public partly subsidizes them. Currently, companies can deduct on their tax returns whatever they pay their executives. To a company paying the top 34 percent corporate tax rate, then, a $1 million salary costs only $660,000. And consumers will often be charged higher prices to cover bloated managerial pay and perks.

To curb the worst of these excesses, shareholders should insist that compensation committees be made up of independent directors; accounting rules should require companies to deduct the cost of stock options from income. The Securities and Exchange Commission has ordered companies to give shareholders a vote on how much executives are paid, and to divulge in their annual reports and proxy statements a CEO's precise total compensation—*and* to explain why it is reasonable.

But much more basic changes are needed. One proposal would disallow business tax deductions for executive salaries in excess of twenty-five times the salary of the lowest-paid employee in the company (as it happens, the salary of the president of the United States is approximately twenty-five times the federal minimum wage), which would still let companies pay their man however much they want—they just wouldn't get a tax subsidy for being extravagant about it.

The Income Discrepancy Act was introduced in the House by Democrat Martin O. Sabo of Minnesota, who argues that his bill would also provide an incentive for executives to raise the salaries of their lowest-paid workers. Twelve percent of adults now living below the poverty line are full-time workers. If they made more on the job, we could save millions of taxpayer dollars in food stamps and support programs like the EITC.

Maybe—just to keep things simple—we should cap the tax deduction for executive compensation at the level of the pay of the president of the United States. If a company thinks one of its officers is worth more than that, let the shareholders pay the cost. Why should you or I subsidize them?

A SHARE ECONOMY

In *The Share Economy*, MIT economist Martin L. Weitzman points out that under the existing fixed-wage system, workers are paid a predetermined piece of the income pie before the pie is even out of the oven. A company's wage bill is independent of the company's health, a system that stabilizes the income of people with jobs but loads unemployment and higher prices—as the higher wages are passed on—on others.

Instead, Weitzman suggests, a larger share of workers' earnings should be paid through a form of revenue sharing. Workers would share a fixed percentage of corporate revenues (with the employer, naturally, receiving the remaining percentage). Companies would then have an incentive to hire new workers, in order to increase production and revenues.

If a large number of major corporations introduced such profit sharing, as each expanded and hired more workers, labor's overall purchasing power would rise; and so, too, would the general demand for goods and services. Thus the idea would:

- reduce unemployment and be a stimulus to the economy during a recession;
- offer a way out of the trade-off between inflation and full employment even when an economy is thriving (because in order to sell the extra output produced by the additional workers, manufacturers would have to hold down prices);

- by establishing a link between corporate performance and labor costs, provide a rationale for a similar link between executive pay and performance.

The big problem here is that part of each individual employee's pay—the part coming from profit sharing—would automatically fall when the number of employees hired by the firm increased. No doubt, this explains why the share-economy concept has gone nowhere fast since it was introduced in the early 1980s.

Much more palatable to workers (and the real key to improved productivity, according to an abundance of studies) is meaningful worker participation *linked to some form of profit or gains sharing*. If each employee is rewarded for the extra effort that worker participation entails with a share of any profits that result, the sky is the limit.

Without gains sharing, worker participation degenerates into Why-tell-the-bosses-anything? What's-in-it-for-us? coffee klatches. And without worker participation, profit sharing is just another way to get paid—the effect on productivity tends to be nil.

At a Whirlpool tooling and plating shop in Benton Harbor, Michigan, a participation–profit sharing arrangement has been in effect since 1988. The bigger the gain in output, the larger the pool of money the workers share with the company. The percentage of the pool going to the workers is determined by the quality of their output, measured by the number of rejected parts. The workers divide their share of the pool evenly, while the company's share is divided between shareholders and consumers—that is, in a balance of profits and prices.

Of course, the Whirlpool workers are taking a risk: If they don't produce more, they don't get paid more. But when the shared-profit scheme was introduced, they were willing to take that chance, for without an improvement in productivity, Whirlpool would have shut down the facility.

Productivity improved. From 1989 to 1991, parts per man-hour were up 10 percent, fewer parts were rejected, and unit costs fell even though wages rose by an average of more than two thousand dollars a year. The company is making more of an effort to teach quality control and to encourage worker initiative, and workers are making more of an effort to cut costs, for all savings go directly into their gain-sharing pool.

The Whirlpool workers' earnings have not risen as fast as their productivity (that lag is what permits the company to stay cost-competitive), but in many other companies, higher productivity and higher profits in 1992 have not been translated into higher wages at all. Gains-sharing agreements can mitigate that kind of exploitation.

So would requiring companies to reveal to employees their unit labor costs, the critical economic determinant of wage competitiveness. Without that information, workers have no way of knowing whether they are getting their fair share of the fruits of increased productivity or just working harder and smarter to benefit shareholders.

The ultimate message, as stated by Fred Block in *Postindustrial Possibilities*, is that "the efficient use of labor increasingly depends on cooperative arrangements between employees and employers that sustain employees' motivation, encourage them to be heard, and assure high levels of investment in the development of their skills."

In the long run, according to Block, productivity and economic growth depend on three things: a firm's commitment to the development of employees' careers, the democratization of decision making, and giving employees a stake in the outcome, through profit or gains sharing or greater stock ownership.

That may sound like a radical utopian dream, but such a

philosophy may be evolving in some of the more developed economies of Asia. In a recent interview, Lee Kuan Yew, the notably nonutopian prime minister of Singapore from 1959 to 1991, explained that "with today's high technology, you just can't squeeze the maximum productivity out of advanced machinery without a self-motivated and self-governing work force. What is the point of having one hundred million dollars' worth of machinery in a factory if you can't get ninety-five percent productivity or more out of it?"

This from the man under whose tutelage Singapore was transformed from a bustling Third World port full of sweatshops to a prototype of East Asian modernization. Take it from the horse's mouth: Worker participation and rising compensation are not just nice ideas; they are the core of a modern economy.

FAIR PLAY DOES PAY

Equal opportunity is rarely seen as important, much less necessary, in maintaining the country's economic competitiveness. Take, for example, the widespread lament that American youth is less well educated than the youth in work forces overseas, a problem that unless corrected will condemn us to declining productivity and a sinking standard of living.

Completely overlooked is the fact that American *women* are better educated and trained than any women in the world. They make up half of all students and degree recipients at all levels of higher education except the doctorate—compared to 42 to 45 percent in major European countries and only 34 percent in Japan.

What's more, American women consistently outperform men academically, starting with high school, in all fields, including engineering, computer science, math, and business.

The problem is that once they hit the male-dominated

offices, factories, and research labs, women run head-on into discrimination. According to a recent study by the Department of Education, by the time they are in their early thirties, women are able to achieve pay equity with men in only seven of thirty-three major occupations—and in five others only if they had earned more than eight credits of college-level mathematics.

Women are also more likely to experience unemployment than men.

It's time to ask what this enduring put-down and under-utilization of trained womanpower is costing in terms of lost productivity and a lower standard of living for us all. We need to beef up the Equal Opportunity Employment Commission (call it the Equal Productivity Commission) and empower U.S. District Attorneys and state attorneys general around the country to pursue discrimination cases aggressively.

Governments at all levels should set a standard for private industry to follow by doing away with harem-style hierarchies. All administrators above a certain grade must be gender representative of the rank and file. Thus, if 80 percent of the teachers in a public school system are women, then 80 percent of the principals ought to be women.

Hillary Clinton once observed that in her tours of Arkansas schools, she had noticed that teachers were almost entirely women, while the principals were usually men—very nice men, she said, "but not educators."

American education, and American productivity in general, might show a measurable improvement if we fully utilized women's talent and enthusiasm, and rewarded them equitably.

MERIT PAY FOR EVERYBODY

If linking pay to performance is a good idea in the private sector, why shouldn't it be in the public sector? How can the federal government ever get a grip on the budget until it has to live with the consequences of the deficit? How can national leaders understand the importance of national productivity until they try to measure their own? Above all, how can they appreciate economic insecurity until they share it?

We should link the salaries of all elected officials to the incomes of their constituents. Thus, if the median income of a congressional district dropped 10 percent, the elected officials representing it would have their salaries cut 10 percent; if the median income went up, only then could the legislators get a pay raise.

If a certain number of districts decline, or the national median income declines, all executive-branch salaries, including the president's, would be cut proportionately.

What about pensions? The average pension received by most people after a lifetime of work is less than seven thousand dollars a year, 25 percent or less of a worker's salary. Retired members of Congress, on the other hand, draw pensions worth up to *276 percent of their last salary while in Congress!* Three convicts who used to be congressmen are still drawing pensions of around 150 percent of their last salary. Make all congressional pensions equal to the average American's and we'd see an immediate appreciation of the utterly inadequate pension system in this country.

We might also link congressional pay to the federal budget deficit. Say, for example, that congressmen's salaries would be cut by $1000 for every $1 billion of red ink that they spill in a year. Or fine them for every $1 billion in spending that they propose without offering legislation that would pay for it.

Congressional pay could go up if the economy was growing. "Put the politicians on commission," comedian Jackie Mason suggested. "Pay them a percentage and you'll see this country's economy grow like Elizabeth Taylor in a bakery."

You may think that's a joke, but Joseph A. Grundfest, an

associate professor of law at Stanford, has seriously suggested tying pay for government officials and civil servants to real GNP growth over a "suitably long period, adjusted to correct for the effects of deficit financing."

The idea makes even more dazzling sense when applied to government forecasters. The Council of Economic Advisers and the Congressional Budget Office routinely generate prognostications on the GNP, employment, inflation, interest rates, and the like, while across the Potomac, the Central Intelligence Agency reads entrails with equal diligence. But the seers in those agencies, as elsewhere, endure pressures to render heavy politically correct readings of the future.

Dr. Grundfest has the perfect free-market solution: Tie a portion of each agency's compensation to its success as an oracle. If the CBO or the CEA does a better job than the Blue Chip forecasters, they get a bonus. If they perform worse, the agency's budget is cut. If the CIA's predictions are better than those of *The New York Times*, the analysts get a reward. If they prove wrong . . . well, the consequences are classified.

NO FREE LUNCH

"Americans are obsessed with rights and entitlements, and I'm not talking about the rights in the Bill of Rights. Americans are demanding rights in every area—gay rights, wheelchair rights, immigrant rights, veteran rights, endangered species rights, suicide rights, right-to-life rights, prisoners' rights, the list goes on interminably. And there are the entitlements—people are entitled to school, three meals a day, pensions, shelter, psychiatric care, medical care, paraplegic care, legal representation, on and on. Funny, everyone talks about rights and entitlements, but there's damn little talk about RESPONSIBILITIES. . . . And the whole syndrome, in my opinion, is messing up this country."

The majority of Americans would probably agree with these comments by Richard Russell, the publisher of the financial newsletter *Dow Theory Letters*. The idea that the recipients of government largesse have obligations in return, that we all need to contribute a little civic effort instead of perennially asking "What's in it for me?" is a deservedly popular notion. It has become a staple on both sides of the political fence, and Bill Clinton gave it a name: the "New Covenant."

The only problem with this laudable return to basic citizenship is that it is not applied widely enough. No one wants to be the one. It is a lot easier to throw money at problems than to ask people how they themselves might solve them, just as it is easier to buy a kid expensive toys than to spend long, patient hours with him or her yourself.

But a society without a sense of common responsibility is as unhealthy as a family without it. So the final idea in this book is that we expand the principle of "rights entail responsibilities" straight across the board, to rich and poor, strong and weak, alike.

■ ■ ■

The most obvious place to begin is Detroit, where the experienced whiners running the auto industry have enjoyed the loving solicitude of government for more than a decade. "Why is it that when government takes care of large industries, its tenderness is called 'tougher trade policy' instead of 'welfare'?" asks columnist Russell Baker. "If New Jersey has a good idea in cutting off added welfare payments to mothers who don't stop having babies, isn't it an equally good idea, if the government starts subsidizing the auto industry, to cut the subsidy every time car tycoons conclude a losing year by giving themselves a pay raise?"

But why stop there? Let's pretend that all the welfare kings and queens among us, from day laborers to the Forbes 400, have to do something public-spirited in return for their government handouts.

- Corporate tax breaks, including all investment tax credits and credits given to Employee Stock Ownership Plans, have to be *earned*. No tax subsidies should be given to companies with twenty or more employees unless the company has a mechanism to give workers a voice in production decisions and a share in financial gains. Such compensation schemes have been shown to increase productivity.
- American drug companies enjoy some of the fattest corporate tax breaks in existence while they have been raising their prices three times faster than the rate of inflation. American consumers pay up to six times more than Canadians or Europeans for the same drugs. Either drug prices should be indexed to inflation, or the companies should lose their special tax write-offs.
- The farm price support system costs the Treasury roughly $13 billion a year, and costs consumers another $10 billion in higher food prices. The bulk of the federal subsidy benefits only 200,000 of the 2.2 million farms in the United States—individuals and corporations that tend to be far wealthier than the average American family.

  These payments must be cut, but in the meantime, all recipients should be obliged to tithe a portion of their production to programs to feed the hungry.
- Banks, which enjoy federal deposit insurance and the use of federal funds at low interest rates, should have to allocate a portion of their loans to local enterprises and home buyers, as required by law.
- Pension funds, in return for their exemption from

federal income taxes, should have to invest a portion of their assets—at least 1 percent—in affordable housing.

- The Resolution Trust Corporation should channel more of the real estate once owned by failed S&Ls to people who need housing—the same people who are paying for the bail-out. By the spring of 1992, only forty thousand dwelling units for low- and moderate-income people had been salvaged out of the debris of the S&Ls' speculation—roughly 1 percent of the needed affordable housing units.

- In return for their license to broadcast into our homes, the commercial television networks should be required to offer at least one hour a day of children's educational programming, and should be penalized (through disallowed ad time) for every act of violence they broadcast. It's time to get tough with a business that wouldn't exist without a public license.

- Every company that denies its employees, full- or part-time, proportional benefits of health insurance, paid sick leave, pensions, or vacations will be ineligible for federal contracts and tax subsidies.

If you like the idea of cracking down on "welfare cheats," think up your own outrageous examples and send them to your legislators along with a copy of this list. Say that you are a member of the "Rights and Responsibilities" movement. And send a copy of your ideas to the publisher of this book, so we can include them in any follow-ups.

TRICKLE-DOWN DRIES UP

For most of the postwar period, the prevailing party line has been that Americans needn't worry about the gap between rich and poor; all we need to concern ourselves with is economic growth, and we'll all get richer together. This notion has been expressed in a number of metaphors: A rising tide lifts all boats; the bigger the pie, the bigger the slices; give hay to the horses and you'll feed the birds. Any way you describe it, it's the trickle-down theory.

Fortunately for us all, the theory was largely correct for almost forty years. Economic growth in the United States *was* good to everyone, and went hand in hand with an overall decline in poverty. As a result, despite its lingering inequities, the country has been spared the squabbles over fairness and distribution that have wreaked havoc in unequal and slow-growing economies like El Salvador and India.

This amiable state of affairs has ended in the United States. An ominous new era dawned during the booming 1980s. Although the economy grew almost as much as it had during the 1960s, and unemployment fell by five full percentage points, not a dent was made in the official poverty rate. In fact, while poverty shrank by a quarter during the palmy sixties, the fast-growing Reagan years ended with a *higher* poverty rate than in 1979. And despite stout efforts to revive the old 1950s sentiment, "What's good for General Motors is good for the country," who could believe that when G.M. jobs were moving to Mexico?

Since 1969, real average weekly earnings have fallen by more than 12 percent, dragging down the income growth of the bottom *70 percent* of wage earners. Even with both husband and wife working, the income of the bottom 40 percent of families actually *declined* during the 1980s. The number of poor people is the highest since 1964, when President Lyndon B. Johnson declared war on poverty.

Meanwhile, it is no secret where all the money made in the 1980s went. Along with crack and designer rice, the decade brought us the first significant rise in inequalities of wealth since the 1920s. By one calculation, the wealthiest 1 percent of American families enjoyed a real pretax income gain of 77 percent between 1977 and 1989. During that same time, the median pretax income of the typical American family rose 4 percent.

By the end of the 1980s, the typical family earned around $36,000 a year, compared with an average income of $560,000 for the top 1 percent. That means that two friends, one who went to Wall Street in 1980 and the other who became a college professor, were in two different economic classes ten years later. While one struggled to pay for basic necessities, the other may well have had three or four servants, a second house in Aspen or Vail, trips to Europe for long weekends, and a new consciousness of privilege.

Clearly, something turned off the tap and stopped the trickle-down.

So our task for the 1990s is manifold. We must figure out how to become more productive. Anyone who understands the power of compound interest can understand the importance of the rate of growth to an economy.

Mainstream American economists point out that if the United States had had the same productivity gains in the 1970s and 1980s that it had in the 1950s and 1960s, we'd have had 40 percent more income—$12,000 to $15,000—per family today.

But even if we do achieve those rates of growth again, it is not at all clear, as the experience of the 1980s showed, that the loaves and fishes would in fact be distributed to every family. And productivity and growth can lose their constituency mighty fast if the goodies stay stuck at the top. Unless we do something to ensure a fairer distribution of economic gains, we may see the evolution of a Third World America, complete with class divisions, class resentments, and class warfare.

But is there a reason to believe that economic equity may

be economically *efficient* as well as politically desirable? Since the birth of capitalism, we have understood that the rewards of enterprise go to those who earn them. The engine of productivity is fueled by the promise of individual reward, and over time this can lead to inequality—the price we pay for economic efficiency.

Economists have also known for a long time that in many highly competitive fields, small differences in ability can translate into large differences in economic reward, particularly in fields like entertainment, the arts, professional sports, and high-level medicine and law. But what happens when these so-called "winner take all" markets, in which a handful of participants reap a disproportionate share of the total rewards, become an increasingly significant part of the economy?

This is what happened during the 1980s, according to economists Robert H. Frank of Duke University and Philip J. Cook of Cornell, who assert that winner-take-all markets have spread substantially in recent years, particularly into investment banking and corporate management, to the point where they may be undermining the overall allocative efficiency of the economy. Too much talent has been encouraged to flock into too few lucrative markets at the expense of other fields of endeavor, like science, where there are great potential gains for society but less financial reward. In other words, there is a brain drain from productive and useful endeavors into fields where "the private value of the prizes will significantly overstate their social value."

When pay distributions become much more highly skewed than the underlying distributions of effort and ability, society is likely to try to alter these arrangements in the name of fairness.

As it happens, that might be just the thing the economy doctor ordered. "The effect of [a progressive] tax will be to shift labor to the production sector, where it will increase aggregate output," Professors Frank and Cook suggest, adding that "in economies where winner-take-all effects are important, the standard claim that progressive taxation comes at the expense of economic efficiency may be false. Output not only need not fall with increases in the tax rates on high incomes, it may very well rise sharply."

There it is—an economic assertion that the alleged trade-off between equity and efficiency is nothing but a fig leaf, a cover for the age-old struggle for the domination of wealth.

Fairness is not a luxury, something that would be nice to have once we get our economic house back in order. We may never have our house in order unless we figure out how to make the system work better for everyone. Perhaps these hopeful ideas can provide a start.

Notes
on Sources

INTRODUCTION

The quote from William Greider on page xx is from his book *Who Will Tell the People* (New York: Simon & Schuster, 1992).

I. TWO WAYS TO CURE THE DEFICIT

Raise Taxes: What the Politicians Aren't Telling You

Much of the material in this chapter, on the revenue-raising effects of various changes in the tax code, comes from the Congressional Budget Office publication *Reducing the Deficit: Spending and Revenue Options*, published in February 1992. The CBO is also the primary source for the changes in the tax rates on various income groups during the 1980s cited on pages 1–2.

For the relative tax burdens of different countries, the source is the Organization for Economic Cooperation and Development (OECD), in Paris (page 1; page 4).

Robert S. McIntyre, director of Citizens for Tax Justice, was an invaluable help in unraveling some of the intricacies of corporate taxation, particularly the potential impact of changes in taxation of multinational corporations and U.S. companies establishing plants out of the country (pages 8–10), and the cost to the Treasury of the net-operating-loss deduction (pages 11–12). *Growth and Equity: Tax Policy Challenges for the 1990s*, published by Citizens for Tax Justice in 1990, provides a good overview of tax policy from a progressive point of view.

Citizens for Tax Justice is supported by labor unions and public-interest and grass-roots citizens groups. The organization's offices are in a shabby third-floor walk-up with peeling paint around the door, in a small building adjacent to the headquarters of the SEIU, the Service Employees International Union (AFL–CIO), which represents janitors and others who haven't had much influence on tax or any other economic matters. The contrast of these premises with the temples of granite and marble, glass and polished brass, where the high priests of the Washington tax bar practice their magic could not be more stark. But McIntyre more than makes up in expertise and integrity what he lacks in decor. He has obviously not sold those valuable assets to the highest bidder.

America: What Went Wrong?, by Donald L. Barlett and James B. Steele (Kansas City, Missouri: Andrews and McMeel, 1992), the best-selling critique of economic developments in the 1980s, also contains a discussion of various corporate tax breaks.

For the section on energy taxes (pages 13–17), I especially relied on work done by the World Resources Institute, a highly regarded nonprofit environmental-policy organization based in Washington, D.C. The description of pollution and traffic-congestion charges and the carbon tax comes from congressional testimony by Roger C. Dower, head of WRI's energy and pollution program, and Robert Repetto, vice president and senior economist of WRI.

The "feebate" idea (page 16) originated with Amory Lovins of the Rocky Mountain Institute in Snowmass, Colorado.

The idea of taxing capital gains on the basis of the time an investment was held and of exempting some of the gains from a new, job-creating business (pages 20–21) was initiated by Senator Dale Bumpers (Dem.-Arkansas), and a version of this was advocated by Bill Clinton. In the interest of full disclosure, I must also note that my husband, John Henry, who was the founder and chief executive officer of a biotechnology company during the 1980s, has long advocated such a change in capital-gains taxation, and so argued at meetings sponsored by the Council on Competitiveness, whose final report supported a similar idea.

We no longer hold stock in the company, which had more than a hundred employees in 1991. When we sold out after ten white-knuckled years, we paid the same capital-gains tax that we would have paid if we had made the profit by buying and selling the stock on the same day.

Cut Spending: Stopping Washington's Checks Before It's Too Late

Neil Howe of the National Taxpayers' Union Foundation in Washington, D.C., and Phillip Longman of *Florida Trend* magazine are responsible for most of the analysis on pages 27–29 on how to structure a fair means test for entitlements. Their views are cogently presented in a piece in *Atlantic* (April 1992). Howe also coauthored a book in 1988 called *On Borrowed Time: How the Growth in Entitlements Spending Threatens America's Future.*

The "4 percent solution" (pages 30–31) has been put forward by the Heritage Foundation, a conservative policy organization located at 214 Massachusetts Avenue N.E., Washington, D.C. 20002 (202-546-4400).

II. HOW TO INVEST A VICTORY DIVIDEND

A New G.I. Bill

Information on the original G.I. Bill (pages 39–40) can be found in *A Call to Civic Service*, by Charles C. Moskos, a professor of sociology at Northwestern University (a Twentieth-Century Fund book published by The Free Press in 1988).

Individual Training Accounts (ITAs) for higher education or for displaced workers (pages 42–43) were proposed by Pat Choate in *The High-Flex Society* (New York: Alfred A. Knopf, 1988).

The "Equity Investment in America Program" (pages 43–44), a plan to finance universal higher education through the Social Security Trust Fund, is outlined in *Financing Opportunity for Post-Secondary Education in the U.S.: The Equity Investment in America Program*, a June 1990 briefing paper written for the Economic Policy Institute by Barry Bluestone of the University of Massachusetts, John Havens and Alan Clayton-Matthews of Boston College, and Howard Young of the University of Michigan. EPI, which is supported by labor unions, is usually described as a liberal economic think tank. It is located at 1730 Rhode Island Avenue N.W., Suite 812, Washington, D.C. 20036 (202-775-8810).

III. HOW TO REBUILD THE COUNTRY

The American Investment Bank (pages 57–58) was first proposed by Jesse Jackson in various speeches and policy papers during the 1988 presidential election campaign. One of the authors of Jackson's "national investment program" was Carol O'Cleireacain, now the finance commissioner for New York City. More recently, New York investment banker Felix Rohatyn of Lazard Frères has been advocating a similar infrastructure investment program, in articles for *The New York Review of Books* (June 25, 1992) and the *Washington Post* (July 6, 1992).

Let Private Money Pave the Way

Other ways of financing needed public investments (pages 59–60) are cited in "How to Restore Long-Term Prosperity in the United States and Overcome the Contained Depression of the 1990s," by S. Jay Levy and David Levy of the Jerome Levy Economics Institute of Bard College (February 15, 1992); and in an article by Pat Choate, "Out of the Ruins," published by the Public Policy Center of the University of Denver in September 1992.

No More Hippie Accounting

The same sources have described the advantages of establishing a federal capital budget (pages 60–62).

The People's Money

A good discussion of the benefits of "economically targeted" investing by public pension funds (pages 62–68) can be found in "Pension Funds and Social Investment," by Carol O'Cleireacain, in the Winter 1991 issue of *Dissent*. A case against such "capital allocations," which has always been anathema to the Federal Reserve, is made in the Spring 1992 issue of the *Regional Review* of the Federal Reserve Bank of Boston ("Public Pension Do's and Don'ts," by Steven A. Sass).

IV. HEALTH CARE: THE BEST SOLUTIONS

The managed-competition concept for health care (pages 73–75) is described in a series of policy documents ("Market Reform and Universal Coverage") produced by Alain Enthoven of Stanford University for the Jackson Hole Group. For information on the single insurer, Canadian-style approach (pages 75–77), contact Physicians for a National Health Program, Suite 500, 332 South Michigan Avenue, Chicago, Illinois 60604.

A description of the "play-or-pay" approach (page 77), along with a sweeping set of proposals for containing health-care costs, appears in the report of the National Leadership Coalition for Health Care Reform, *Excellent Health Care for All Americans at a Reasonable Cost* (November 1991). The Coalition, including major corporations and former presidents Carter and Ford, is based in Washington, D.C. (202-637-6830).

Other cost-cutting reports have been prepared recently by the General Accounting Office and the Rand Corporation, among others.

V. CHILDREN: IT'S THEIR TURN

The Kindest Cut

The most thoroughgoing recent review of children's issues was published in 1991 by the National Commission on Children, which provided the basis for some of the legislative proposals now before Congress, including the Refundable Children's Tax Credit (pages 84–87). For other information and policy recommendations concerning children, nothing surpasses the publications of the Children's Defense Fund in Washington, D.C.

The historic figures on the children's tax credit (page 85) are based on work by economist Eugene Steuerle of the Urban Institute.

Another excellent report on children's issues is called *Putting Children First: A Progressive Family Policy for the 1990s*, by Elaine Ciulla Kamarck and William A. Galston, published by the Progressive Policy Institute. The Institute, an economic research group affiliated with the Democratic Leadership Council, by its own account advocates "growth-oriented" economic policies that go beyond the conventional left-right debate. It is located at 316 Pennsylvania Avenue S.E., Suite 555, Washington, D.C. 20003 (202-547-0099).

I am also indebted to Robert Greenstein, director of the Center on Budget and Policy Priorities in Washington, D.C., for the phrase "the kindest cut" (page 83), which he used as the title of an article in *The American Prospect* (Fall 1991).

VI. EDUCATION: THE BEST CHOICES

The charter-school concept (pages 94–98) originated in Minnesota and is best described by Ted Kolderie in a series of publications put out by the Public Services Design Project of the Center for Policy Studies in St. Paul (612-224-9703). Note in particular "The Charter Schools Idea" (June 19, 1992).

The Great Training Robbery

The specifics of the apprenticeship idea (pages 104–108) are based on European models and on two reports: *America's Choice: High Skills or Low Wages!*, the report of the Commission on the Skills of the American Workforce (National Center on Education and the Economy, June 1990), and on a paper prepared for the Progressive Policy Institute by Robert I. Lerman of American University and Hillard Pouncey of Swarthmore College and Brandeis University, entitled *Why America Should Develop a Youth Apprenticeship System* (March 1990).

VII. VOLUNTEERING

National Service

The national volunteer service is described in the Moskos book *A Call to Civic Service*, cited above.

VIII. THE BANKS: HOW TO CREATE A DEMOCRATIC MONEY SYSTEM

For ideas on how to reform the banking system, the best place to begin is with the Financial Democracy Campaign. The organization's headquarters are at 604 West Chapel Hill Street, Durham, North Carolina 27702 (919-419-1841 or 687-4004); the FDC also has an office at 729 8th Street S.E., Washington, D.C. 20003 (202-547-9292).

FDC's founder, Tom Schlesinger, director of the Southern Finance Project, can be contacted at 329 Rensselaer, Charlotte, North Carolina 28203 (704-372-7072).

ACORN (Association of Community Organizations for Reform Now) has a home office at 523 West 15th Street, Little Rock, Arkansas 72202 (501-376-7151). Executive director Steven Kest can be contacted at 845 Flatbush Avenue, Brooklyn, New York (718-693-6700).

Charlie Mac

The banking expert quoted on page 127 is Robert Litan of the Brookings Institution. Litan is not sympathetic to the populist program of the Financial Democracy Campaign, but he does believe that poor neighborhoods need better access to bank credit, which could be expanded by means of a public secondary mortgage agency like the suggested "Charlie Mac."

A Central Bank for Community Lenders

The proposal to turn the Federal Home Loan Bank system into a source of financing for community lenders (pages 129–30) was described in congressional testimony by Elena Hanggi, director of the Institute for Social Justice, Little Rock, Arkansas, before the Subcommittee on Housing and Community Development of the House Banking Committee (June 10, 1992).

No More Bank Bailouts: How to Reform Deposit Insurance

The outline for deposit insurance reform (pages 131–33) is from *No More Bank Bailouts*, by Jane D'Arista, an associate director of the Morin Center for Banking Law Studies at the Boston University School of Law. Ms. D'Arista was also for many years an economist with the House Banking Committee of the U.S. House of Representatives. The paper was published as a briefing paper by the Economic Policy Institute in 1992.

IX. A NEW DEAL FOR SMALL COMPANIES

Filling the Capital Gap

A description of the Michigan Strategic Fund's "capital access" program (pages 135–36) is found in *The Entrepreneurial Economy Review*

(October 1988), published by the Corporation for Enterprise Development, a nonprofit group providing ideas and assistance to organizations concerned with increasing economic opportunity through entrepreneurship. The CED is located at 777 North Capital Street N.W., Washington, D.C. 20002 (202-408-9788).

Doug Ross, who as director of Michigan's Department of Commerce from 1984 to 1989 was instrumental in developing an innovative and widely acclaimed economic-development strategy in that state, is now at Michigan Futures, 38777 West Six Mile Road, Livonia, Michigan 48152 (313-953-1010).

Another source of information on the capital-access and similar programs is Steven Rohde, formerly of the Michigan Strategic Fund and now with the consulting firm of Hansen, McOuat, Hamrin & Rohde, 700 13th Street N.W., Suite 950, Washington, D.C. 20005 (202-434-4558).

An Industrial-Extension Service

The idea for an industrial-extension service (pages 136–39) is described in *Modernizing Manufacturing*, by Philip Shapira, published by the Economic Policy Institute in 1990.

Company Networking

Many of the ideas about manufacturing networks (pages 139–41) are detailed in the Autumn 1990 issue of *The Entrepreneurial Economy Review* published by the Corporation for Enterprise Development.

X. HOUSING: HOW TO PUT A ROOF OVER EVERY HEAD

The Jacuzzi Subsidy

Many of the figures on the mortgage-interest tax deduction (page 144) are from a 1992 study done by economist James M. Poterba of the Massachusetts Institute of Technology.

A 15 percent cap on mortgage-interest deductions was suggested in a 1991 report produced by the Twentieth-Century Fund's task force on affordable housing. The New York–based research foundation said that the housing needs of the "poor and near-poor" should be met by "redirecting" some of the billions spent on homeowners' tax breaks.

In Land We Trust

For more information on community land trusts (pages 145–48), contact the Institute for Community Economics, 57 School Street, Springfield, Massachusetts, 01105-1331 (413-746-8660).

Two nonprofit housing groups that have been widely praised for their efforts in providing low-income housing are the Enterprise Foundation in Baltimore, Maryland, which was started with the help of developer Jim Rouse; and Habitat for Humanity (1-800-HABITAT), which builds affordable homes in partnership with low-income families worldwide. Habitat's most famous volunteer: former president Jimmy Carter.

XI. CONSUMER POWER

Citizen Utility Boards

The Citizen Utility Boards: Because Utilities Bear Watching, by Beth Givens, provides an excellent description of the CUB movement (pages 151–52). The book was published by the Center for Public Interest Law of the University of San Diego Law School in 1991. For further information on similar groups, the best sources are the consumer organizations that developed out of Ralph Nader's efforts. Most large states, including Alaska, Arizona, Colorado, Connecticut, California, Florida, Illinois, Maryland, Massachusetts, Michigan, Minnesota, Missouri, Montana, New Jersey, Ohio, Oregon, Pennsylvania, Washington, and Wisconsin, have a Public Interest Research Group (PIRG); the national headquarters of the USPIRG is at 215 Pennsylvania Avenue S.E., Washington, D.C. (202-546-9707). USPIRG's grass-roots campaign office is located at 312 Pennsylvania Avenue S.E., Washington, D.C. (202-546-3965).

A Financial Consumers' Association

If you are interested in organizing an FCA initiative (pages 154–55) in your state, contact one of the U.S. Public Interest Research Groups or Public Citizen, Ralph Nader's organization, at 2000 P Street N.W., Washington, D.C. 20036 (202-833-3000). If you live in a smaller state, in which mailings might not generate enough revenue to sustain a viable CUB or FCA, find out if the state has an intervenor compensation program. If it does, you may qualify for funds if you can demonstrate that your group can represent the public interest in financial regulatory proceedings.

The Ten-Minute Citizen

If you want to join Working Assets (pages 156–58), call 415-788-0777.

XII. COMMUNITY POWER

How to Fight Back

An excellent source of information on various state and city laws on plant closings has been published by the Federation for Industrial Retention and Renewal. Called *State and Local Initiatives on Development Subsidies and Plant Closings*, it analyzes all known state and city experiences with plant-closing laws and laws that protect taxpayer interests when companies receive development subsidies. The book is available from FIRR at 3411 W. Diversey Avenue, #10, Chicago, Illinois 60647 (312-252-7676). Since January 1989 the Federation has also published a newsletter, called *NEWS*, which describes various community efforts to counter the economic dislocation associated with plant shutdowns (pages 160–67).

Greg Leroy of the Midwest Center for Labor Research is a living repository of similar information. The Center (312-278-5418) is located at the FIRR address.

A new project, the Guild Law Center (formally known as the Maurice and Jane Sugar Law Center for Economic and Social Justice, 2915 Cadillac Tower, Detroit, Michigan 48226 [313-962-6540]), is becoming a national clearinghouse for legal assistance in the battles against plant closings.

What You Can Do

For information on the "Plant-Closing Dirty Dozen" (pages 174–75), contact the Federation of Industrial Retention and Renewal. The address of the Coalition for Justice in the Maquiladoras (pages 175–76) is c/o Interfaith Center on Corporate Responsibility, Room 566, 475 Riverside Drive, New York, New York, 10015 (212-870-2295).

XIII. YOU CAN TAKE YOUR PENSION WITH YOU

Some of the data on the shrinkage of private pension coverage (pages 177–78) is from "The Fall in Private Pension Coverage in the U.S.," a study by David E. Bloom of Columbia University and Richard B. Freeman of Harvard University, published in the 1992 proceedings of the American Economics Association.

America: What Went Wrong also contains a discussion of the inadequacy and decline of private pensions in the United States.

The portable-pension-plan solution (pages 180–81) is proposed in *The High-Flex Society*, by Pat Choate (New York: Alfred A. Knopf, 1988). The idea of a mandatory universal pension system (MUPS), financed by mandatory contributions to individual accounts similar to 401K plans, was studied in the 1970s. A description of this and other provocative thoughts about the pension system are found in *Labor's Capital: The Economics and Politics of Private Pensions*, by Teresa Ghilarducci (Cambridge, Mass.: MIT Press, 1992).

XIV. WHAT TO DO ABOUT WELFARE

A Stake in the System

The concept of an Individual Development Account (pages 183–84) to enable most Americans to build assets has been developed by Michael Sherraden of the School of Social Work at Washington University in St. Louis. Many of the details are described in his article "Rethinking Social Welfare: Toward Assets" (*Social Policy*, Winter 1988) and in a policy report entitled "Stakeholding: A New Direction in Social Policy," put out by the Progressive Policy Institute in January 1990.

Sacred Bulls

The problem of runaway fathers received a great deal of publicity and attention during 1992, in everything from the popular press to the Clinton platform. Actual solutions are still in short supply. If you are a working parent who needs help in collecting court-ordered child-support payments, you can contact Dennis Bannon of Children Support Services in Laurel, Maryland (301-470-4294), which takes cases or refers them around the country; or Charles Drake in San Antonio, Texas, who has helped set up child-support-collection agencies throughout the United States. Children Support Services is part of an informal seventeen-state network of private agencies that share information on missing parents.

Microlending

For a brief overview of microlending (pages 187–91), see *Microenterprise: Human Reconstruction in America's Inner Cities*, a June 1991 policy report for the Progressive Policy Institute by Lewis D. Solomon, a professor of law at George Washington University. For more information on how to start and operate a program, through a foundation, a church, a nonprofit organization, or a local government agency, contact Robert Friedman, Association for Enterprise Opportunity (415-495-2333), or Cathy Kelley, Women Venture (612-646-3808).

A Family Wage

Some of the most recent data on the effects of an increased minimum wage (pages 191–93) have been developed by William E. Spriggs for the Economic Policy Institute in Washington. For an analysis of the Earned Income Tax Credit (pages 193–94), I relied on a paper by Robert J. Shapiro of the Progressive Policy Institute, which supports an expansion of the EITC and opposes an increase in the minimum wage.

In *Who Will Tell the People*, Bill Greider suggests that PPI's position is influenced by the fact that several wealthy businessmen finance the Institute and sit on its board. Among them is Robert Kogod, president of the Charles E. Smith Company, a Washington real-estate firm that at the time (1991) paid its cleaning workers $4.75 an hour, with an extra quarter an hour for cleaning toilets.

The company was struck by the D.C. janitors' union and finally changed its labor policies after several rabbis in the Washington area expressed their support for the janitors. But the rabbis' stance had not, at last report, persuaded the Progressive Policy Institute to support an increase in the minimum wage.

By mentioning these connections, Greider violated one of the unwritten social codes of Washington. It is not considered polite to inquire whether someone's public-policy position has any relationship to who pays their bills.

XV. GROWTH AND EQUITY:
TWO SIDES OF THE SAME COIN

A Share Economy

An enormous literature exists on the productivity effects of various forms of worker compensation (pages 199–202). One place to start is *Paying for Productivity*, published by the Brookings Institution in 1990, edited by Alan S. Blinder. The major and unexpected finding in this series of papers was that whatever the form of compensation, meaningful worker participation enhances productivity. Some scholars would add that worker participation cannot be "meaningful" unless it is rewarded with a fair share of the gains stemming from productivity improvements, a characteristic notably absent from the American economy in 1992.

For a provocative discussion of the kinds of alternative, more democratic working arrangements that could produce greater economic growth, see *Postindustrial Possibilities: A Critique of Economic Discourse*, by Fred Block (Berkeley and Los Angeles: University of California Press, 1990).

Index